NEW HORIZONS IN CRIMINOLOGY

A CRIMINOLOGY OF POLICING AND SECURITY FRONTIERS

Randy K. Lippert and Kevin Walby

BRISTOL
UNIVERSITY
PRESS

First published in Great Britain in 2019 by

Bristol University Press
University of Bristol
1-9 Old Park Hill
Bristol
BS2 8BB
UK
t: +44 (0)117 954 5940
bup-info@bristol.ac.uk
www.bristoluniversitypress.co.uk

North America office:
Bristol University Press
c/o The University of Chicago Press
1427 East 60th Street
Chicago, IL 60637, USA
t: +1 773 702 7700
f: +1 773-702-9756
sales@press.uchicago.edu
www.press.uchicago.edu

© Bristol University Press 2019

British Library Cataloguing in Publication Data
A catalogue record for this book is available from the British Library

Library of Congress Cataloging-in-Publication Data
A catalog record for this book has been requested

ISBN 978-1-5292-0248-9 hardcover
ISBN 978-1-5292-0250-2 ePub
ISBN 978-1-5292-0249-6 Mobi
ISBN 978-1-5292-0246-5 ePdf

The right of Randy K. Lippert and Kevin Walby to be identified as authors of this work has
been asserted by them in accordance with the Copyright, Designs and Patents Act 1988.

Cover design by blu inc
Front cover image: istock
Printed and bound in Great Britain by CPI Group (UK) Ltd,
Croydon, CR0 4YY
Bristol University Press uses environmentally responsible print
partners

For Bruno Ujevic

Contents

Notes on authors

Randy K. Lippert is Professor of Criminology at University of Windsor, Canada, specialising in policing, security, and governance. Previous publications include *Condo Conquest* (2019) and *Policing Cities* (2013) (with K. Walby).

Kevin Walby is Chancellor's Research Chair and Associate Professor of Criminal Justice at the University of Winnipeg, Canada. Previous publications include *National Security, Surveillance, and Terror* (2017) (with R. Lippert) and *Corporate Security in the 21st Century* (2014) (with R. Lippert).

Acknowledgements

We would like to thank Mathew Zaia, Curtis Labute, and Bilguundari Enkhtugs for their attention to detail and helpful efforts. We would also like to thank Rebecca Tomlinson from BUP and Andrew Millie for their hard work in bringing this book to fruition.

Some of the thoughts in *A Criminology of Policing and Security Frontiers* have been developed from work in our previous books and articles. We would like to thank all of our colleagues who have been involved in other publications:

Chapter Two is a significantly reduced, augmented and revised version of Lippert, R., Walby, K. and Wilkinson, B. (2016) 'Spins, stall and shutdowns: Pitfalls of qualitative policing and security research', Forum: Qualitative Social Research, 17(3).

Chapter Four draws on the article below and is significantly revised and reduced: Walby, K. and Lippert, R. (2012) 'Spatial regulation, dispersal, and the aesthetics of the city: conservation officer policing of homeless people in Ottawa, Canada', *Antipode*, 44(3): 1015–33.

Chapter Five is partially based upon: Sleiman, M and Lippert, R. (2010) 'Downton ambassadors, police relations and "clean and safe" security', *Policing & Society*, 20(3): 316–35.

Chapter Six is partially based upon: Walby, K. and Lippert, R.K. (2012) 'The new keys to the city: uploading corporate security and threat discourse into Canadian municipal governments', *Crime, Law and Social Change*, 58(4): 437–55.

Acknowledgements

NEW HORIZONS IN CRIMINOLOGY

Series editor: Professor Andrew Millie, Department of Law and Criminology, Edge Hill University, UK

Preface

A Criminology of Policing and Security Frontiers by Randy K. Lippert and Kevin Walby is the seventh title in the New Horizons in Criminology book series. All books in the series are by leading authors and reflect cutting-edge thought and theoretical developments in criminology. This title is no different. Over the past decade Lippert and Walby have developed a strong reputation for their work on urban policing and security. Their work takes a broad definition of policing and introduces readers to areas of policing and security that are less often the focus of mainstream policing research (e.g. Lippert and Walby, 2013; Walby and Lippert, 2014; 2015). In this book they push the frontiers of policing scholarship even further. The authors take the concept of 'frontier' to mean "the edge and realms beyond conventional policing and security thinking and practice". Examples of frontiers that they consider include the private funding of public police, and the work of ambassador patrols, conservation officers and corporate security personnel. The authors note that such examples may be dismissed as they are most often associated with the visible deterrence of nuisances, anti-social behaviours or minor rule violations, whereas the public police also deal with more significant criminal or terrorist threats. But such dismissal would be a mistake – not, as the authors say, because they support "the now debunked 'broken windows' thesis", but because of the disproportionate impact on disadvantaged populations often identified as perpetrators.

Lippert and Walby consider temporal frontiers with different agencies working at different times of day or night, at different speeds, tempos, or pace; and spatial frontiers, including post-colonial understandings of the frontier, something that has resonance in the authors' home country of Canada (as well as elsewhere). In popular imagination the frontier is a place outside the law's reach. The authors argue that the frontier in twenty-first century policing and security is not "a 'wild west' devoid of oversight"; yet it can be a place where resourcing blurs boundaries between public and private. Lippert and Walby are interested in how ambassadors, corporate security personnel, community safety officers, and conservation officers are involved in cleaning up the frontier, in preserving an aesthetic through various forms of physical and social cleansing. As the authors note in the conclusions to this book, "The downtown must be clean as well as safe, parks must be free of real and human 'garbage', and so too must fronts of government buildings retain a clean image, as dismissed employees accused of a corporate infraction are escorted out the backdoor by corporate security personnel".

Gaining research access to these new frontiers is not always straightforward and Lippert and Walby make good use of freedom of information requests. They demonstrate that criminology should not regard public police officers as archetypes of policing, nor should we see contract security as the epitome of private security provision. Policing and security is far more complicated and interwoven than this simple dichotomy suggests, and especially so on such new frontiers of practice.

This book is highly recommended. It provides challenges to conventional understandings of policing and security. And by focusing on frontiers, it casts light on areas of practice not often seen and pushes theoretical understandings of a blurred world of plural policing and security provision.

References

Walby, K. and Lippert, R. (2015) *Municipal Corporate Security in International Context*, Abingdon: Routledge.

Walby, K. and Lippert, R. (eds.) (2014) *Corporate Security in the 21st Century: Theory and Practice in International Perspective*, Basingstoke: Palgrave Macmillan.

Lippert, R. and Walby, K. (eds.) (2013) *Policing Cities: Urban Securitization and Regulation in a 21st Century World*, Abingdon: Routledge.

ONE

Introduction: Policing and Security Frontiers

Policing and security are subjects that are central to criminology. Much criminological attention is paid to public police as well as contract private security agencies and guards. Yet there are emergent and other neglected forms of police and security provision on the frontiers of scholarship and practice. These range from brightly coloured ambassador patrols engaging urbanites on the streets, to community safety officers removing graffiti and quelling nuisances just beyond main police beats, to conservation officers walking obscure trails to look for homeless people's camps in the farthest reaches of urban parks, to mostly hidden corporate security personnel in public government, and to public police sponsors drawn from private corporations operating in the shadows.

The idea of the 'next frontier' in policing or law enforcement is often invoked to signify something historically unique. Several criminologists have invoked the notion of frontier but usually only descriptively to refer to a space (McDonald, 1995; Hayward, 2004; McCulloch, 2004; Scott et al, 2007; Carrington et al, 2010). So it begs the question, what should 'frontier' mean for criminology and for studies of policing and security?

Geographers and political scientists have long distinguished geopolitical frontiers from borders (Newman, 2003, 2006), the latter denoting a rigid, clear-cut nation-state boundary. Since the 1990s, a multidisciplinary critical border studies literature has emerged to challenge a static definition of the border (Kolossov, 2005; Parker and Vaughan-Williams, 2012; Brambilla, 2015). For example, Brambilla (2015: 15) identifies a 'move away from' borders 'as naturalised and static territorial lines', arguing for a notion of 'borderscapes', one of several notions that share some features with the notion of frontier, but nonetheless differ from it (see Geiger, 2009). Critical geographers have sought to decouple the notion of frontier from colonial historical accounts of 'settler societies' and 'American exceptionalism', arguing the 'frontier notion was ethnocentric in the extreme' (Geiger, 2009: 17) and reclaim it as a general analytical concept although one which keeps reference to the nation-state. While geographers have written on frontiers, they have rarely provided in these accounts direct and detailed focus on policing and security practices. A frontier is more mobile, less secured and more ambiguous than a traditionally understood border. It is a realm adjacent or beyond a border and decidedly more ephemeral. Thus, Geiger (2009: 1) asserts that frontiers are 'loosely-administered spaces rich in resources'.

Elsewhere, frontier refers to ambiguous and shifting landscapes and encounters (Naum, 2010). In a useful discussion, Kristof (1959: 270) argues that the frontier is characteristically defined as the space in advance of a formal border, 'the beginning ("forehead") of the state; it was the spearhead of light and knowledge expanding into the realm of darkness and of the unknown'. Kristof (1959: 271) continues, noting that the frontier is often treated as 'both a source of danger and a coveted prize'. He proceeds to underscore that the frontier is a space without total, effective state control and is absent of widely accepted laws.

Although Kristof's (1959) comments are oriented to the scale of the nation-state or international relations, he provides useful language for elaborating on the frontier theme. Spatially, the frontier is ahead or in front of formal spaces of control. Danger and reward are assumed to emanate from this uncertain space. Little policing and security scholarship has pursued an analytical understanding of frontiers (Bigo, 2005; also see Giacomantonio, 2014). Notably, Lamb et al (2018) have advanced the notion of police 'frontierism' to explain the varied work (containment, confrontation, conversion and conquest) that police undertake at numerous social and geographic boundaries. Yet, temporally, the frontier is the future, where action could happen too. Control and law are never quite complete here. In this book, we approach the frontier as an organising theme and an entendre not limited to spatial connotations. We endeavour to use the complex frontier theme in ways that are relevant to criminologists and scholars in criminal justice, critical security and socio-legal studies. Our understanding of the frontier theme has threefold, overlapping meanings:

- First, frontier means the edge and realms beyond conventional policing and security thinking and practice. Each form of policing and security provision elaborated in this book is operating on such a frontier in a vital way. We investigate these novel and neglected developments at micro and organisational scales, but the exact kinds of agents, logics and resources making their work possible on these frontiers should not be assumed in advance.

- Second, frontier refers to how these forms of policing and security are taken up by scholars in ways beyond or across clear-cut disciplinary boundaries. Chapters draw on some concepts not immediately or traditionally associated with criminology, and use theoretical and methodological tools developed in sociology.
- Third, the frontier has a specific meaning in colonial countries such as Canada and Australia, where state formation involved violence and assimilation targeting Indigenous people (Monaghan, 2013). Nettelbeck and Smandych (2010) reveal that colonial police used the idea of a frontier to animate their attempts to control Indigenous groups and usurp their sovereignty and access to land. The idea of frontier plays a central role in Australia's national imaginary (Nettelbeck, 2011) as well as in Canada and the United States (US). For Monaghan, writing on Canada, 'the frontier is a milieu to be ordered' and in this way it animates 'within the frontier ... policing and security strategies that are established to anticipate, contain, and control outbreaks of perceived dangers' (Monaghan, 2013: 124). Indeed, this frontier theme is still found in privately funded official narratives of public police museums, as we show in Chapter Seven. The spaces where this oft-violent policing occurred were regularly termed 'the frontier', and this historical context shapes policing and security practices to this day. The policing and security agents and practices we examine are often called upon to engage Indigenous peoples, a re-enactment of these colonial frontier relations with significant implications for justice and inequality. The notion of frontier is relevant today in urban realms in informing policing and security provision that often detrimentally affects other disadvantaged groups that include other youth, homeless people, and racialised minorities too, justifying practices in complex ways as though it were an older colonial frontier. This colonial dimension of the frontier makes types of policing and security provision possible.

In this book, we are trying less to use frontier as a concept and more to fill this organising theme with analytical meaning related to policing and security, and the spatial and temporal dimensions in which they happen. The book's empirical scope includes public corporate security officers, conservation officers, community safety officers, ambassador patrols, 'paid duty' and private foundation funding of public police in Canada and the US, but with relevance to the United Kingdom (UK), Europe and Australia – and sometimes with global purchase – as these practices and ideas migrate further as part of the diffusion of policing and urban security policies. What becomes popular on the policing and security frontier, perhaps especially in the US, can spread to other regions. The now largely discredited idea of 'broken windows' and zero tolerance public policing (Harcourt, 2005) is a prime example of this tendency (Lippert and Walby, 2013).

We seek to show criminology cannot remain narrowly fixated on public police as typical of policing or on contract security guards as the epitome of private security provision. Nor can criminology assume that these two forms provide the key distinction between public and private spheres. Policing and security has become, and perhaps always was, far more diverse and complex. Such a narrow focus risks leaving criminology a conceptually and empirically impoverished field, unable to make sense of what is happening on the frontiers of thinking and practice. Criminology should be pushed to the edge of its current understandings to theorise and examine the shifting landscapes of policing and security practice. When criminology arrives at the edge and adopts the notion of frontier, it reveals previously hidden or less elaborated insights about policing and security provision (see Chapter Eight). Some previous research and theoretical reflection on policing and security based in geography, socio-legal studies or sociology results in similar research and concepts that talk past one another (Lippert and Walby, 2013). Few accounts explicitly acknowledge overlap among empirical interests, methods and theoretical concerns of other disciplines. The frontier notion encourages thinking about how these barriers can be hurdled to foster greater cross-disciplinary thinking and empirical analyses of policing and security, because it avoids the idea of firm boundaries.

We strive to highlight the value of interdisciplinary work as we tackle the themes of this book. Besides the anchoring theme of frontier, this book has three other major themes:

- The first is this notion of engaging with concepts from beyond criminology to provide a more persuasive and nuanced framework for understanding new or neglected forms of policing and security provision. Analysis needs to break free of standard disciplinary confines into conceptual frontiers.
- Second, we explore new, even edgy methods such as freedom of information (FOI) requests to travel to and through these frontiers and spot pitfalls to avoid along the way. We push criminology to the limit of its current methodological, qualitative frameworks.
- Third, policing and security policies and practices entail migration and often diffusion of ideas and practices, for example from the US to Canada, or from the UK to Canada and Australia. This happens

in ways that make national borders increasingly irrelevant and which we examine to show how policing frontiers are constantly advanced.

Our primary aim is to explore neglected or under-researched and historically novel policing and security developments, by drawing on recent empirical qualitative research. The book contributes to criminology as a field of study, by expanding understandings of policing and security, opening up new avenues of research, and drawing on other disciplines to expand and update its conceptual and methodological repertoire. We believe that criminology focused on these frontiers must open itself up to conceptual and methodological innovations, by both looking through new windows at disciplines from which it has been curtained and opening previously locked doors between disciplines. This does not mean – to continue with this metaphor – tearing down load-bearing walls of the criminology house so the roof caves in because there is nothing distinctive left to hold it up as a discipline. Rather, we want to open windows and doors to let fresh ideas into criminology, to avoid being stifled by old ways, with the aim of better understanding shifts, invention, dissolution and contestation of contemporary policing and security provision.

Most of the chapters that follow use interviews with policing and security agents or related users and supporters of their practices and/ or materials acquired through FOI requests. Interviews provide rich insider views that are impossible to gain through most other means. FOI is a cutting-edge way of producing empirical material for analysis and it is brought to bear here on policing and security provision (Walby and Larsen, 2012). Researchers can make FOI requests in countries around the globe (over 100 at the time of writing) that have access laws. Savage and Burrows (2007) call on scholars to rethink the repertoires of social science knowledge production, which will require methodological innovation. We think FOI can be part of this initiative. Our methodological reflections on how to push the boundaries of criminological research thus have international resonance. Some chapters are supplemented with relevant mass media accounts too. All chapters are informed by recent empirical research. Our investigation and analysis of policing and security frontiers is also longitudinal, since we have examined each realm for five to 10 years, using qualitative methods.

Policing and security provision are fast evolving and mutating. The concepts we use in this book range from dispersal (Chapter Four), to 'clean and safe' logic (Chapter Five), to credentialism (Chapter Six), and come from sub-disciplines and literatures that represent cutting-edge thought. Almost all chapters pertain to newer types of policing and security work that, while taken up in Canada, and/or in Canada and the US, were transferred from one nation to another, will likely migrate soon, or have operated in several countries but are neglected in scholarship. This transfer or diffusion is not a side issue, but instead is central to the notion of frontier. Chapters that follow also remark upon practices in other countries such as the UK and Australia, where appropriate, to demonstrate how these frontiers come from or whether they have entailed policy transfer and mutation. *A Criminology of Policing and Security Frontiers* seeks to make conceptual, methodological and empirical contributions to policing and security studies – and to criminology more broadly – for international scholarly audiences.

Chapter outlines

The book's chapters are organised as follows. This introduction lays out the book's themes, concepts and arguments. We first describe what we mean by the notion of policing and security frontiers. Again, a frontier, unlike a border, is not immobile, secured and plainly demarcated; rather, a frontier lies adjacent to – or spatially and temporally beyond – a border. In each chapter we remark, where appropriate, how frontier has threefold, overlapping meanings.

Chapter Two is about getting to and over the frontier, and focuses on methodologies developed to accomplish this travel. If policing and security policies are transferred and mutate, we need methodologies that discern the contours of this migration. To accomplish this feat, we explore elements of qualitative research on policing and security agents on the frontiers of thinking and practice. We focus especially on FOI requests as a cutting-edge method. This chapter also discusses common barriers encountered on the way to frontiers. While it is often assumed that policing and security agencies and agents, including those working on frontiers, are difficult to access due to their bureaucratic, secretive or obscure nature, this chapter argues that this is not necessarily true. Yet, getting to the frontiers of policing and security is not without pitfalls. These pitfalls are like falling into risk categories – ironically like those sometimes used by policing and security agents in their own work. The chapter concludes with methodological strategies for scholars to avoid these pitfalls and, ultimately, to advance research that aims to interrogate policing and security frontiers.

Chapter Three takes up community safety officers (CSOs), transitional agents who are linked to public police, and more broadly considers community policing frontiers. Community policing now has a long history across national borders. CSOs have been prominent local security providers in the UK, Australia and elsewhere for two decades. In the UK, CSOs and related neighbourhood policing emerged from reassurance policing that was partially influenced by earlier US ideas on community policing. Currently in the UK, austerity is challenging the continuation of these kinds of policing, and yet these models are influencing developments beyond its borders. Examining recent establishment of CSOs in cities in Western Canada, this chapter engages in international comparative research at the frontier of community policing. We analyse FOI disclosures and policy documents to demonstrate that CSO establishment in Canada has not involved a straightforward transfer of criminal justice policy from the UK to Canada. Instead, there have been policy mutations, notably when the Royal Canadian Mounted Police (RCMP) implemented a pilot CSO program in several cities, but in other instances too. We show that CSO development in Western Canada has been deemed to have mixed results, but CSOs are nonetheless currently being touted as a supplement to municipal public policing in Ontario, Canada's largest jurisdiction. Examining CSO programs and practices in Canada contributes to international literature on CSOs, to debates about reassurance and community policing, as well as to understanding the peculiar ambiguity of community policing that exists in many countries.

Chapter Four confronts conservation officers, dispersal and urban frontiers. It examines National Capital Commission (NCC) conservation officers' regulation of homeless people, many of them Indigenous people, in Canada's capital city, Ottawa. Conservation officers are a neglected form of security provision. We explore NCC officer practices, by analysing occurrence reports obtained through FOI requests and interview transcripts. The officers are also called upon to regulate Indigenous peoples in these park spaces. We contend that policing of NCC parks is organised by a logic of dispersal. Such policing aims to preserve an aesthetic for public consumption and ceremonial nationalism, entails specific temporalities, and is made possible through a policing and security network. Dispersal more accurately conceptualises the spatial regulation here compared with alternative concepts like banishment, and therefore supplements existing typologies of spatial regulation. We conclude with a discussion of these typologies for future research on urban policing and regulation and the notion of frontiers. There is a sense in which they reproduce the colonial dimension of the frontier in how they approach these peoples.

Chapter Five examines agents on more visible city centre or downtown frontiers. This chapter investigates uniformed patrols called 'ambassadors', who are increasingly providing security in the nooks and crannies of city centre cores across many countries. These programmes migrated from US cities like Baltimore and Philadelphia to cities in Canada, then to the UK cities, and far beyond, and are intimately connected with urban 'revitalisation' and mostly class-based gentrification strategies. While discussing the New York Police Department (NYPD) in this regard, geographer Neil Smith (1996) aptly called this gentrification the 'new urban frontier'. Interviews with public police and ambassadors in three Canadian cities reveal that ambassador operations and practices are shaped and made possible by relations with police that entail exchanging knowledge for limited training and tacit tolerance. Ambassadors are imagined remaining distant from police and private security self-designations and appearances to the benefit of police and business improvement districts (and similar organisations), but not so remote as to lose vital benefits of these links. Ambassadors act as police 'eyes and ears' and govern 'nuisance', using indirect and unauthorised strategies. In these arrangements, ambassadors are not so much 'steered' by police as 'anchored', suggesting notions of 'networked governance'. In some Canadian cities, these patrols are called upon to regulate Indigenous peoples on the city centre frontier. These patrols can be seen beyond North America too. Making sense of ambassador practices and relations with police is accomplished through reference to a 'clean and safe' logic that positions ambassadors as its agents – and sometimes its targets too.

Chapter Six examines another new kind of policing and security agent – public corporate security personnel – with attention to the frontiers of security knowledge and credentialism. This chapter explores the establishment of corporate security units in municipal and federal levels of government in Canada. By drawing on analysis of FOI requests, and interviews with corporate security agents, we show how corporate security, operating in the private sphere, is now entering new and unexpected frontiers to become elements of policing and security networks. This chapter focuses on how knowledge and technology from the American Society for Industrial Security (ASIS International) is transferred into Canadian levels of government and their newer corporate security units and operations as well as into the UK and Australia through some of its 240 chapters worldwide. Public corporate security entails logics of asset protection, risk and liability management, employee surveillance, and order maintenance, and that these are enacted by migration of this increasingly prized ASIS knowledge and credentials into new realms. We discuss the implications of our analysis of public corporate security for understanding policing, security and public accountability as well as frontiers.

Chapter Seven considers the longstanding but surprisingly neglected 'user pays'[1] policing, as well as newer and proliferating police foundations in Canada and the US. As in other chapters, we draw from analysis of FOI disclosures and interviews to examine these trends and developments in North American jurisdictions. We begin by describing the scope and reach of this kind of policing, followed by detailed analysis of the kinds of users and perceptions of this practice. We also document the migration of police foundations from the US to Canada and foundation activities. This is accomplished, in part, by a discussion about foundations and police museum narratives and absences regarding frontiers. These developments are a new funding frontier in North American policing and security that we compare to the trend of austerity in the UK. The chapter concludes by raising questions about these practices for public accountability in western countries.

This book concludes by identifying seven subthemes, derived from exploring policing and security frontiers, for future research and for criminology as a field of study. These are:

- nuisance
- aesthetics
- public police relations
- the role of law
- moving resources
- oversight
- contestation.

One main frontier highlighted here is positioned between public and private realms. There is a sense in which the forms of policing and security described in the foregoing chapters defy this boundary – in myriad ways – the most. We conclude the chapter by advocating adoption of this book's themes for future research and thinking in criminology and suggesting that greater attention be paid to forms of policing and security neglected due to methodological myopia and stagnation as well as to fixed disciplinary boundaries.

Notes

[1] This is also termed 'extra duty', 'special duty', 'paid detail', 'paid duty' and 'secondary employment', depending on the public police department.

TWO

Getting to the Frontiers: Methodologies

Introduction

Policing and security research has increased dramatically in the past two decades. This has happened across disciplines in which qualitative inquiry is prevalent, including criminology. Simultaneously, the reach and scope of existing policing and security agencies has been widening, often through new laws granting greater powers of search, surveillance, arrest and detention beyond their traditional purview (Ericson, 2007; Earl, 2009). Some agencies and agents remain understudied despite long histories; many other new ones have yet to be studied. On police and security frontiers, the agencies are becoming more networked and are increasingly collaborating and sharing information that identifies risky spaces and persons consistent with their evolving and sometimes expanding mandates.

This chapter is about getting to policing and security frontiers, and it focuses on methodologies developed to accomplish this travel. We explore elements of qualitative research on policing and security agents on frontiers of thinking and practice. This includes freedom of information (FOI) requests, which are a cutting-edge method and thus befitting research on frontiers.[1] The chapter discusses ways of accessing and moving on to frontiers to study forms of policing and security elaborated in other chapters, as well as common barriers encountered on the way and strategies to circumvent them. While it is often assumed that policing and security agencies and agents, including those operating on frontiers, are difficult to access due to their clandestine, bureaucratic or obscure nature, this chapter argues that this is not necessarily the case. Unlike the Northwest Mounted Police's much celebrated Great March West to a Canadian frontier, the subject of numerous books and even police museums (see Chapter Seven), and repeated in other colonial nations consistent with their mythologies, getting to policing and security frontiers is far chancier and more mundane for researchers. It is less a grand, straight-line, disciplined march, and more an improvisational dance. If, as Greene

(2014) puts it, research on and with policing (and security) agencies is like trying to master the tango, then the growing networking and reach of these agencies is adding erratic beats and requiring fancier footwork among researchers to be allowed into their frontier dancehalls.

The question is how best to approach and access these agencies and agents, since, as we show, studying them involves unique challenges. Such research is challenging from the outset because all policing and security agencies (and related knowledge and funding transfers) tend to be secret, secured or otherwise difficult to access by scholars interested in how they operate, through what rationales, with what effects, and how these aspects may be shifting. As famously noted by Max Weber (1946 [1922]), state bureaucracies have this propensity for secrets, as do private corporations (Penders et al, 2009). These challenges are like those found in other public and private agencies or organisations, such as private corporations, which have been accessed through special arrangements and strategies contemplated and advocated by researchers (Penders et al, 2009). Research on other criminal justice agencies, such as prisons, has documented similar blockages and barriers (Martel, 2004).

Policing and security agencies are well equipped to be secretive, sometimes taking this to extremes, because they can use security to avoid scrutiny whenever deemed useful. This means police and security personnel are sometimes not only reluctant respondents (Adler and Adler, 2002), but also trained to evade questioning or avoid full disclosure when participating in research. We think these agencies deserve special attention. In view of these challenges and dynamics, we ask pressing questions for qualitative policing and security researchers:

- How best can researchers access policing and security agencies and their practices and relations on frontiers?
- Once in, how does one avoid getting drawn or falling into the risk categories that are the stock and trade of these agencies?
- What kinds of pitfalls are encountered, and what happens when one falls in?
- How can qualitative researchers step over or climb out?

The questions asked by qualitative researchers differ from those of quantitative researchers in demanding greater access to internal workings and nuances of the agencies that quantitative data rarely reveals on its own. By attempting to answer these questions, this chapter contributes to qualitative research literature on policing and security practices (Hoogenboom and Punch, 2012; Aradau et al, 2014).

Policing and security agencies are often presumed to be hard to access due to their enclosed nature (for example, behind a blue wall). However, we argue that access may be no more onerous than for other public organisations. This chapter reveals that for two distinct qualitative projects in Canada, access was gained to policing and security services. Our experiences also demonstrate, however, that this access and research is not without pitfalls. Inspired by contributions that call for honest accounts of the trials and tribulations of the qualitative research process (Tracey, 2010), we identify three kinds of pitfalls encountered in these projects. We term these 'security spins', 'security stalls' and 'security shutdowns'. These were experienced in relation to three qualitative methods: field/ethnographic research, personal interviews, and informal and formal FOI requests. We used multiple strategies for producing data because of acknowledged limits to knowing in qualitative research (Doucet and Mauthner, 2008) and the attendant need for triangulation (Harari and Beaty, 1990). Traditional questionnaire research with police and security personnel may explore attitudes, but often does not fully reveal the organisation of policing and security strategies and practices over time. Yet with triangulation it becomes trickier to interpret data (Moran-Ellis et al, 2006), and pitfalls emerge that can threaten project completion. These pitfalls stem from how policing and security agents and agencies manage risk in their routines.

First, we review literature on access in police research and elaborate our notions of security spins, security stalls and security shutdowns. Then we examine data and field notes that illustrate these challenges and barriers, and how we managed them in a Canadian context. Our analysis adds to debates on strategies for research access, recruitment and sampling in qualitative research (Malachowski, 2015). Finally, we discuss strategies for policing and security scholars contemplating similar qualitative research and how best to avoid these pitfalls on their way to studying new frontiers.

Challenges in qualitative research on policing and security

Literature on qualitative studies of policing organisations (Alison et al, 2001; Cockcroft, 2005) has examined issues of information management and the challenges of working with secretive agencies. Of course, classic ethnographic studies of policing by Bittner (1970), Manning (1977) and Ericson (1981), among others, are foundational for police studies. However, security agencies, including those discussed in this book, differ from public police. Different challenges in negotiating access can arise, depending on the topic or method used. New contributions that explore research methods in security studies (Aradau et al, 2014; Lisle, 2014) have explained discursive and ethnographic approaches to qualitative research in the post-September 11 era. Yet few contributions in this policing and security literature have considered the routine ways that research access is mitigated and blocked, especially not from a perspective that entails multiple data production strategies.

Seeking access to policing and security agencies is varied in aspiration and scope. For two research projects in this chapter, sometimes the aim was merely to access documents representative of agency practices or that described a subset of agency programmes. Other times it involved accessing personnel for face-to-face, semi-structured interviews about their agencies' activities and occasionally telephone interviews when preferred by personnel. In one instance, discerning how public police departments' past was represented and funded entailed visiting museums devoted to each department and which were said to be open to the public. While it might seem an easy way to enter this frontier, it was soon discovered that many 'open' public police museums were located *inside* the police department's physical headquarters. Thus they required passage through at least one and sometimes two or three levels of security. In one instance, this included undergoing a pat down and metal detection screening, and in all cases providing photo identification that was copied and presumably stored by the police department.

Building a broader dataset also at times entailed accessing agencies over a longer term and following agents around during their work as shadows (De Leon and Cohen, 2005; McDonald, 2005). Contrary to expectations regarding the nature of policing and security agencies, access was gained to security agents in the field, including our projects. This was achieved even though we are outsiders who conduct critical, academic research (see Thomas, 2014 for a discussion of types of police researchers). Our position on policing and security practices by the agencies we researched is, first, that what is practised in the name of 'security' has grown considerably, especially since 11 September 2001. Sometimes practices termed 'security' are an effort to 'govern through security'; that is, using security as an excuse or pretext, wittingly or unwittingly, to accomplish all manner of outcomes, some contrary to the public good or which are otherwise unaccountable (Walby and Lippert, 2015a).

Through carefully crafted request letters, emails, telephone calls and meetings, along with continuous researcher image self-management involving careful consideration of how one refers to oneself leading up to the field, we gained access to most agencies we approached. This was accompanied by promises of confidentiality and sharing of research results where relevant. These issues of rapport and trust are important in qualitative research (Corbin and Morse, 2003; Kaiser, 2009), especially with police (Brewer, 1990).[2] In many respects, these agencies were no different than other public organisations; many were willing to participate after our research aims were outlined and safeguards put in place. But the process was not without pitfalls, nor can it be approached any old way. What makes these policing and security agencies distinct is that risk management is central to what they do (Ericson and Haggerty, 1997; Walby and Lippert, 2015a); they are experts at identifying and managing risk, thus doing research about them is fraught with potential problems.

We have encountered many kinds of pitfalls on the way to policing and security frontiers; ours is not an exhaustive list. In reflecting on our experiences in two projects, three types stand out: security spins, security stalls and security shutdowns.

Security spins

We define a *security spin* as an effort to redirect or reshape the meaning of claims, observations and practices of a policing or security agency for the inquiring researcher. The notion of spin recognises that these agencies compete for recognition (Walby and Lippert, 2015a) and for funding from, in these instances, public sources and political or administrative masters. It also connotes the idea that rather than a straight-line march to the frontier, one should expect to be periodically spun off course or diverted in a slightly new direction. Claims or practices of these agencies, if their meaning is not reworked, risk damaging reputations and reducing the funding flow (management of reputations to sustain police legitimacy, as we argue in Chapter Seven, is also permitted on new funding frontiers). These spins are an effort to manage identified reputational risks (also see Haggerty, 2004).

Of course, other public agencies have designated spin doctors attending to an organisation's needs and providing remedies. Certainly, participants are known in qualitative research to misrepresent, pad, massage or rework the truth of the matter. But policing and security personnel themselves, from the chief to a manager or administrator to the lowest level agent patrolling on the ground, can and do represent themselves and their practices in ways that may be more appealing to audiences. Merely because policing and security agencies and agents possess considerable legal powers and tend to operate with little public oversight, we found, does not mean they proceed without concern about reputations (Dupont, 2015).

Security stalls

Security stalls are the second type of pitfall and are of a different order compared to spins. Stalls occur while negotiating access for information from policing and security agencies, as well as after those negotiations are complete and the research has commenced. Stalls seek not to reshape meaning of known policing and security agencies' claims or practices, but instead strive to manage reputational risk temporally, by slowing new information transfer to the researcher, perhaps to buy time to reshape or prepare the information. They might be thought of as an unexpected traffic jam on what was thought to be a freeway to the frontier, bringing everything to a temporary halt.

Stalls also may be presented by bureaucratic barriers, such as the requirement of administrative authorisation, and may be used to manage operational risk, such as labour costs associated with participation (for example, cost of compiling and redacting data, facilitating or participating in research). The former type of stall tends to be used when revealing the information about practices that is legally required, as in FOI requests; and the latter used in considering approval for in-depth access to personnel for interviews or observations. Both types may be used, in hope that the researcher will scale down or abandon the project. With stalls, the researcher may still obtain data, but it requires sustained negotiation (perhaps with multiple sites) and may take so long as to threaten project feasibility or even prevent project completion.

Security shutdowns

Finally, *security shutdowns* are the most serious of the three types and can be impossible to escape. They are the potentially most damaging to research projects, if qualitative scholars fall into them. Here, the policing or security agency has identified risks (for example, to reputation) to be too serious and unruly for spins or stalls to overcome. Shutdowns mean a complete, permanent lockdown of information release. The shutdown decision is also sovereign in character; its rationale need not be communicated to researchers. However, shutdowns tend to pertain to decisions by the immediate agency at only one site, rather than at all similar sites and agencies. They are troubling, because of the possibility that researchers may be blacklisted by others networked to the immediate agency. We describe two shutdowns in this chapter, but neither led to blacklisting. This result may speak to weak ties among agencies on some frontiers, but may also reflect a hesitancy to reveal to other networked agencies that we had accessed the agency or that any information was transferred to us in the first instance.

It requires wit and being reflexive (Guillemin and Gillam, 2004; Riach, 2009) to manage these pitfalls. To promote more reflexive policing and security research, we hope that our accounts make researchers aware of similar dynamics in their efforts to get to the frontiers of policing and security provision.

Pitfalls in corporate security and public police research

We conducted qualitative studies of two kinds of agencies: public corporate security and public police, both of which are discussed in more detail in later chapters. In each case, we engaged several organisations of each type simultaneously, as discussed in this chapter.

Public corporate security

Corporate security units in large private organisations have a long history, especially in North America. Their historic association with union busting, surveillance and violence at the Ford Motor Company in the early 20th century is well known (Weiss, 2014; Walby and Lippert, 2015b). Though tactics have changed, these units have remained. Today there are few, if any, major private corporations without a corporate security office. But in recent years, corporate security values, credentials and practices have begun migrating into various levels of public government (see Chapter Seven). In the first project, we sought to investigate this trend in municipal corporate security (MCS) units in Canadian cities (Walby and Lippert, 2015a). We adopted a research design involving interviews with MCS representatives as well as FOI requests about these units' practices.

We begin with shutdowns. We had been granted interviews with two key MCS personnel, one of whom was a graduate of the university programme in which one researcher taught. We established rapport and there was explicit mention that we could return for in-depth, follow-up research. But several weeks later, our email request for a follow-up interview with these personnel and access to lower-level personnel went unanswered, as did the next three, one of which was directed at another representative in case our contact person had been on leave, transferred or retired from their position. We never heard from them again. This caused concern that other agencies would act similarly or their rationale for this decision, which remains unknown, would be passed to other MCS units. Another MCS unit – this time with surprisingly little effort on our part – provided the access we sought, including shadowing and a focus group with key security personnel.

Another near shutdown we encountered during research occurred inadvertently. One of us was delivering a public talk about security as part of a city walking group tour. The tour was planned to include a short lecture on MCS upon arrival at the city square in Victoria, British Columbia. When pontificating about forms of surveillance that MCS personnel use, their lack of identifying uniforms, and the implications for use of public space, he noticed two MCS personnel deliberately moving through the audience. Members of the audience noticed these agents' presence – their ear buds were something that the second author drew attention to midway through the talk. Several crowd members seemed shaken by the encounter with these MCS personnel. After the two agents walked away, some members criticised their intrusion. In the coming months, the MCS representative from this city was not forthcoming about completing a previously agreed upon interview or granting interview access to MCS personnel. After he retired a year later, when reputational risks were lessened, he agreed to an interview. Though we eventually interviewed other staff, access was permitted only after this lengthy stall.

One mundane but common and telling example of spin comes from an MCS representative being queried about the use of surveillance cameras at City Hall in another city and which we learned we had been subjected to without our knowledge. When asked, the MCS representative spun their purpose as 'security' cameras, insisting that MCS does not conduct surveillance. It was common for corporate security personnel to explain that use of surveillance cameras was not for surveillance but for security. This distinction, which might be lost on those whom the cameras view across municipal properties and parks, downplays privacy concerns associated with surveillance and seeks to manage MCS reputations, by suggesting that they are instead in the business of protecting public safety (see Chapter Six).

Stalls also occurred when examining corporate security at other levels of government. We submitted FOI requests at the provincial and federal levels to numerous departments. At the provincial level, an FOI request was sent to Manitoba Hydro, that province's Crown Corporation responsible for electrical energy. The request was for:

[t]he number and types of investigations carried out by Corporate Security in Manitoba Hydro HQ from April 1, 2011 to July 15, 2014. Sample of official job description and protocol for Corporate Security in Manitoba Hydro. Sample of reports/plans for recent, past projects of Manitoba Hydro Corporate Security. Annual reports of Corporate Security for previous four years. Annual budget and general expenditure list of Manitoba Hydro Corporate Security for previous four years.

This request was mailed to the FOI coordinator for Manitoba Hydro – this was the only designation on the envelope. After some weeks, we telephoned Manitoba Hydro to speak with the FOI coordinator. We then received a response from a representative (who would only identify themselves as a Manitoba Hydro employee) asking for more details about our request. After several days, the person called again, this time revealing they were the corporate security director at Manitoba Hydro and would be responding to the request. We then replied that not only had this run-around delayed the processing of the request, but it had also contravened FOI legislation, since the office of primary interest had been given our request directly and had learned our identity. We explained to this corporate security director that they needed to forward the request to the FOI coordinator, who would be charged with seeing it through. After another two weeks, the FOI coordinator responded and apologised for the poorly developed FOI culture and breach of FOI protocol. The requested information was eventually disclosed.

We submitted similar requests to numerous federal government departments, including the Department of National Defence. Its FOI coordinator stalled the request, by claiming this Department was without a corporate security unit. We engaged in three tense conversations with the coordinator, remarking that all federal government agencies that received the same request had so far indicated that they had such a unit and would comply. Yet this coordinator still insisted that his Department had no such security unit, and indicated he wanted to close the file. We had fallen into a methodological pit, from which we had to escape. So we then spent time locating all open source material we could discover, including policy and budget documents from the Department of National Defence website that revealed the corporate security unit's existence. On receiving this material, the coordinator then chose an unusual course of action, by suggesting we contact the – previously unknown – corporate security unit directly to clarify the parameters of the search. A corporate security unit representative then responded, indicating the requested information was not formatted to fit the parameters of the search as per our original wording and asked for drastic alteration of the request. The representative eventually released some files outside the FOI process. We had found our way out of this pit, although the representative had responded in a way that disclosed information that still suited his agency's interests.

Public police

Public police are increasingly working for private buyers of their services in 'user pays' policing arrangements (see Chapter Seven). This development, along with that of private sponsorship of police, has raised empirical and normative questions about the nature of policing in the early 21st century and whether it serves private interests rather than primarily the public good (Lippert and Walby, 2014). We investigated this practice through interviews with public police officers and FOI requests to police departments. These FOI requests sought to obtain information about users and the character of the relations between officers and users, whom were found to be nightclubs, malls and film production companies (see Chapter Seven).

Four municipal police departments were sent FOI requests about 'user pays' policing – or what is called 'paid duty' in this provincial jurisdiction's parlance. The response varied dramatically in terms of completeness of the disclosure and the speed with which it was made available. But the FOI request encountered a stall from one major police department, whose paid duty practices had received much negative local media and political attention preceding our request. Given this publicity, we think what we describe was informed by the police department's desire to manage reputational risks.

We first mailed an FOI request to the police department's address with the required payment using a postal money order. We requested: 'all logs of paid duty assignments for 2010-11 inclusive'. We indicated that we were not seeking information about which officers took up paid duty assignments, but only about who the users of these services were, assignment duration, time of day, and date from which a typology of users could be discerned through analysis. From the other police departments, we received acknowledgment of similar requests by mail within the required 30 days (often agencies acknowledge and request additional time to prepare records). After several months, no acknowledgment of our request or any other information was received. We had not paid extra to track the envelope or whether the money order was cashed. To receive a formal receipt for the FOI request, the first author travelled to this police department's headquarters in person (a round trip of several hours), in part to resubmit the FOI request, to pay the fee to a cashier in the headquarters' lobby, and to receive the formal receipt.

After waiting several months and not receiving acknowledgment of this second request, we appealed to the Information and Privacy Commissioner of Ontario (IPC) that oversees FOI requests. We indicated in the appeal that we had received the same or similar information from other police departments and the low cost of doing so (CDN$0–$120). We were later instructed by the IPC representative, who then contacted the police department on our behalf, that this police agency now acknowledged receipt of one of the two requests and that their response was forthcoming. They had not acknowledged either request until after our appeal to the IPC. The police then responded in a formal letter that estimated the costs to provide the information. The estimate was for CDN$2,071, many times greater than for similar information from other police departments. This was plainly a further stall. The police department was finally acknowledging our request as required by law, and the existence of our requested information, but the cost of its acquisition was made prohibitive. We again contacted the IPC. Its representative explained we could request that the police department waive this fee according to the legislation, if certain criteria were met. Now, five months after the initial request to the police department, we sent another letter copied to the IPC, which read:

> I am requesting the fees for the Freedom of Information request be waived consistent with subsection 45(4) of the [Municipal Freedom of Information and Protection of Privacy Act] for two reasons:
>
> 4(a) The actual cost of processing, collecting and copying the record is much less than the amount of payment required. Other police departments, including those nearly as large, have provided exactly the same information at a small fraction of the cost that your office at the [police department] has quoted. …
>
> 4(c) The information is being used for non-profit research purposes, the results of which will benefit public safety.

Two and a half months later, we learned in a letter that this police department had denied this request. The rationale given was that each police department 'is a different entity and is not required to keep the same database format'. Interestingly, their letter also indicated: 'Please note, your request dated May 17, 2012 and assigned our file number 12-2015 ... duplicates 666 pages of this request. You may wish to amend your request and ... reduce your fees [your charge] by $799.20'. This meant that the police department, for the first time, had acknowledged that it had received *both* our initial requests and not just one of them. Because of this refusal, the next step was to mediate through the IPC.

During mediation over FOI requests, a public agency is supposed to show the IPC mediator give and take. However, the fact that we had made two requests (that is, the second 'duplicating' the first) rather than one (only necessary because the police agency had ignored the first) was now being used to show movement in its stance on making the information available. The police department used our second request for the same information (a direct result of their refusal to acknowledge our first request) to justify the initial high cost they quoted, and also to show some flexibility. This move was not enough to bring the costs (still almost CDN$1,300) in line with costs of information released by other police agencies. Through 21 email exchanges with the IPC mediator, we decided to reduce our request to only three months of information, to reduce the projected cost. We could do this at this point only because the agency had acknowledged receipt of the request and that the records existed. Two months later, we received an IPC mediator's email, indicating the police department had agreed to provide these records by the next month for CDN$290. However, after making payment with a postal money order, this time tracked to ensure it was received, we still had not received the requested information. For this reason, we contacted the arbitrator yet again, this time via four more emails, almost a full year after we had made the first initial FOI request.

The file then had been transferred to a new IPC representative, to whom the first author sent the following:

> I want to proceed with another appeal since I have paid $290 to [police department] but never received the agreed upon information ... It was supposed to be received by mid–March, according to ... the previous mediator. It is now the end of April. The second half of the payment via a money order has been cashed after April 6th. I have to account ... for the $290. I also would like to know how much longer you expect I will have to wait to receive the information. ...

The IPC representative responded, by indicating that they would commence a 'failure to disclose' appeal. No timeframe or other information was indicated. The next week, we finally received the much-reduced information from the police department by mail.

Strategies to advance qualitative research into policing and security frontiers

Encountering – or falling into – pitfalls on the way to frontiers can be frustrating and troubling, especially when it is known that a spin, stall or shutdown is imminent. Challenges and barriers are part of qualitative research (Malachowski, 2015), which can make the process tedious and emotionally draining (Blee, 1998).

We next elaborate on several strategies for qualitative researchers to seek to avoid or escape the pitfalls derived from our experiences. Tracey (2010) notes that the credibility, coherence, significance and resonance of qualitative research will only be enhanced if researchers are honest about the challenges and failures they encounter. Our account is reflexive to the extent that it evaluates the research process, enables public scrutiny of our research and provides a view of mutual collaboration.

Engaging simultaneously with multiple agencies

One strategy to avoid these pitfalls, which we used, is to engage with multiple policing and security agencies simultaneously. This is important when a spin, stall or shutdown jeopardises the inquiry with one agency. Depending on a researcher's resources (time, funding), this may require approaching numerous agencies at the outset. It may also demand being prepared either to engage all that agree to participate, to withdraw a request once approved, or to approach and engage with alternative research sites, should research pitfalls be encountered. This extra step helps to avoid all three pitfalls and enhances research credibility.

When there are shutdowns, research may continue unabated with other agencies. Though troubling and sometimes inexplicable, at no time did shutdowns threaten an entire research project of ours. At first, we incorporated this step into our research design more on a hunch – or as a pragmatic response to encountering a pitfall. We advocate designing this step into research, to ensure that if one information stream dries up on the trip through the frontier, others continue to flow.

However, this strategy is dependent upon the selection (or sampling) of agencies of interest. The feasibility of this strategy requires that there be enough such agencies at a study's outset. For us, local public police organisations and corporate security units in government were relatively plentiful; there were many from which to invite participation and still permit pursuit of our research questions. The population from which to sample would not necessarily be as large for all policing and security research (or similar research with few such organisations from which to select). Qualitative research focused on *federal* public police organisations would be different, since there are relatively few, so this strategy would be unavailable to overcome the three kinds of pitfalls.

Using multiple qualitative methods

A second strategy is to design research projects that draw upon multiple qualitative methods. This is often referred to as 'triangulation', but need not be limited to three methods. Again, this mitigates any spins, stalls or shutdowns that an agency might use against any specific method, and enhances credibility and significance of the research.

Though we accessed many agencies in our three projects, several simply denied access or prevented use of one method (such as interviews or document collection). Alternative and (what we have claimed are) cutting-edge methods (for example, FOI requests) allowed for continued data collection. We discovered that there is often little communication between the recipients of the different methods. FOI staff do not necessarily communicate with field agents, and sometimes the information gathered for a disclosure has not necessarily involved alerting a manager who might be interviewed later. However, researchers should use caution – if a key manager or others become aware of the FOI request, this could damage rapport or encourage spin, stalls or even a shutdown.

Further, for FOI requests it makes sense to simultaneously access different sites whenever possible, even if it means reminding some personnel of the requirements (or existence) of FOI legislation. Disclosures can be wildly variable – from what seems like a full disclosure (though one can never know for certain) to a few pages of information, and every amount in between. Yet, based on full (or almost full) disclosures, it becomes possible to infer the existence of similar documents in other agencies.

Researchers can also identify patterns and logics of agencies' selection for release of documents this way. Some agencies may not release currently politically contentious information. However, others may not be experiencing this public controversy and may readily make similar documents available. This strategy reduces the likelihood of a shutdown across agencies. This also involves, where necessary during stalls, a strategy of revealing that FOI requests with similar agencies yielded all (or most) of the requested information, shaming an agency for not complying with legislative requirements or peer practices.

Merely because a police agency thwarted this strategy in one instance mentioned earlier in this chapter does not mean that it was ineffective. Rather, because the agency was compelled to respond to it – and some information was obtained through IPC mediation – suggests that this strategy may have worked.

In anticipation of shutdowns and stalls as pitfalls, research design should also include data production strategies that may seem only tangentially related to primary research questions at the outset. Researchers should also use appeals at other sites as a strategy to encourage agencies to disclose more information. The use of multiple qualitative methods also permits researchers to recognise spin in specific agencies.

Gaining outsiders' perspectives

A related third strategy is to include participants from outside the agency, but who are nonetheless networked with that agency. In public corporate security contexts, private security personnel contracted to perform guard duties sometimes agreed to be interviewed. This strategy can allow researchers to gain outsiders' perspectives on an agency's practices, where the compulsion to change the meaning of the agency's practices is absent or, since they might also be concerned with the network's reputation, is at least less likely. By incorporating multiple methods and by including outsiders' perspectives, researchers can mitigate the effects of spins on the way to the frontier.

Contacting the right person in the organisation

A fourth strategy concerns preventing stalls in negotiating access and disclosure with agency personnel. The formal representative of any large organisation (for example, a municipal government or police department public relations representative) has more resources at their disposal and often more experience. They should be avoided as a first point of contact. This is because there is no way to gauge the autonomy of any given policing and security representative or unit (or department within a larger organisation) beforehand. Nothing is necessarily gained by entering an agency at much higher levels. Starting at the top is neither always advantageous for research success, nor does it necessarily safeguard research participants from harm by protecting confidentiality or anonymity.

When ethics boards blithely recommend doing this, it may simply be what Haggerty (2004) calls 'ethics creep'. By this term, he means the increasing governance of research using risk categories (that in policing and security research all too easily dovetail with risk categories that policing and security agencies themselves use) (see also Prior, 2010; Burr and Reynolds, 2012).

One strategy is to contact department representatives or middle managers whenever possible and to let them decide whether they need approval (while strictly adhering to ethics requirements – which may require working with one's own ethics board to ensure that access need not be brokered through organisational heads). When negotiating access with these agencies, critical researchers may also wish to ensure that their discourse is middle-of-the-road, especially on the telephone during recruitment. This is not deception, since ethics protocols are being followed. Rather, it is an anti-confessional approach to negotiating entry to field sites – what we referred to earlier in this chapter as 'researcher image self-management'. Such management is no more deceptive than the everyday construction of our selves; not everything in our past, current and future back stage accounts can be revealed by pulling open a curtain during initial interactions with strangers on the telephone or in personal encounters (Goffman, 1959). Given the secrecy of policing and security agencies (Adler and Adler, 2002), it is best to follow paths leading into frontiers of policing and security that are least apt to foment the pitfalls of stall and spin.

Conclusions

This chapter has identified three types of pitfalls in qualitative research about policing and security agencies that we have labelled spins, stalls and shutdowns. We have illustrated these pitfalls in two policing and security research contexts. Policing and security agencies are deserving of special reflection due to their use of security to keep practices secret and their power over the citizenry.

We then proposed strategies to overcome such barriers in this specific area of qualitative inquiry and in other research that targets other, especially public, organisations. These strategies are important for researchers to consider for future research since, despite tremendous growth in the reach and power of policing and security agencies on the frontier, there has not been a concomitant growth of research that explores their inner workings and relations.

One parting point about gaining access to policing and security agencies under study is important to note. The extent to which access to the frontier is denied is the extent to which there is cause for concern about what policing and security agencies are doing to populations they watch and control (Earl, 2009). The stakes are high. More wit and innovation in negotiating access and greater use of investigative research tactics may be warranted, because of the potential for unwarranted secrecy by these agencies. Moreover, we think that such approaches are justifiable, when studying powerful new and neglected agencies. We take up this point in subsequent chapters. These are situational decisions that each researcher must make, weighing up ethics on the books or in policy against relational ethics (Guillemin and Gillam, 2004) and the growing need to illuminate policing and security practices that are potentially: undemocratic; wasteful of precious public resources; reducing the life chances (via criminalisation or exclusion) of Indigenous and other disadvantaged groups; and even unlawful.

In subsequent chapters, our research illuminates these overlooked agencies or the purposely darkened spaces – ravines, alleys, backrooms and obscure private sites on the frontier. Where these strategies work, it may represent one of only a few remaining means to satisfy this need and to serve the broader public good. The tactics required – and the fact that, as outsiders, we gained access to and were sometimes welcomed by these agencies – can serve as a measure of their transparency and accountability.

Notes

[1] For the Canadian federal government, as well as other jurisdictions, freedom of information is called 'access to information', but we use the abbreviation FOI for simplicity here.

[2] There is not enough space to examine issues of identity, power and access in police and security research (for example Belur, 2014). We recognise that gender, for instance, is a key aspect of interview encounters (Schwalbe and Wolkomir, 2001) and is pertinent for us because White men dominate the corporate security sector (Walby and Lippert, 2015a).

THREE

Community Safety Officers and the British Invasion: Community Policing Frontiers

Introduction

Community safety officers (CSOs) have emerged as local security providers in a dozen Canadian cities since 2001. First developed in the UK, the CSO model has been since transferred to Australia too (Cherney and Sutton, 2004). CSOs are not private security agents, since they are public employees of municipalities and other levels of government. Despite being publicly funded, CSOs are not public police either, because they lack key police powers and don dissimilar uniforms. CSOs conduct active patrols in downtown areas and other neighbourhoods as a form of reassurance policing (Barker and Crawford, 2013) and community policing (Brogden and Nijhar, 2005; Fielding and Innes, 2006; Lambert et al, 2012). They tend to operate according to the 'broken windows' thesis (Wilson and Kelling, 1982; Harcourt, 2005) that seeks to remove visible signs of disorder. As a result, CSOs in Canada have also become responsible for multiple practices, including regulation of nuisance and anti-graffiti campaigns.

CSOs operate in Western Canadian cities that lack a public police department or receive minimal Royal Canadian Mounted Police (RCMP) service.[1] They are also expanding where local public police are said to require additional support. No scholarship has examined why these CSOs have emerged in Canada, how local policing and security provision are impacted, or the international policy connections that CSOs may have in Canada. In the UK, CSOs were first introduced via New Labour legislation (Crawford and Lister, 2004; Hughes and Gilling, 2004). In 1998, local governments were mandated by the Home Office 'to develop local partnerships with strategies for reducing crime and disorder' (Gilling and Hughes, 2002: 5). For Canadian CSOs, the principal knowledge transfer stimulus has been CSOs in England. Some Canadian CSOs have emerged independently of public police, but the RCMP also has created a CSO programme to enhance visible presence in towns where regular RCMP officers cannot conduct high-cost patrols. Whether CSOs in Canada differ from CSOs elsewhere has not been examined.

Like the conservation officers and ambassadors we reflect on in other chapters, in many ways CSOs are being called upon to manage conduct at the frontier of crime that is merely disruptive or out of place. In this sense, they represent a frontier of policing practice. They are also called on to work in urban frontiers. The role that CSOs play in local security networks, how CSOs have diffused among Canadian municipalities and the variation in CSO practices also remain unknown. This dearth of empirical research restricts academic understandings of security, safety, and reassurance and community policing in Canadian jurisdictions and elsewhere (Bazemore and Griffiths, 2004; Fielding and Innes, 2006; Monaghan, 2008; Lambert et al, 2012; Barker and Crawford, 2013). Gilling (2001: 395) argues more research is needed on CSOs internationally to discern whether multiple CSO models in the UK have been transferred to new sites. For Gilling, community safety is 'an international policy development' (2001: 382) and research is needed outside the UK.

This chapter focuses on:

- CSO programme establishment and expansion in Canada from 2001 to 2014;
- CSO practices, including patrols, surveillance, policing of municipal lands, and cooperation with agencies in local networks;
- the role of international CSOs in transferring policy to Canada.

We argue that the establishment of CSOs in Western Canada was not a straightforward exercise in international criminal justice policy emulation. Instead, policy mutation happened not with the initial CSO policy uptake in Canada, but instead as CSOs entered the RCMP's purview and other Canadian jurisdictions. We demonstrate too that introduction and expansion of CSOs in Canada is an indicator of the status of reassurance and community policing in Canada that competes with alternative models, such as municipal corporate security transferred from the private sector and ASIS International (the American Society for Industrial Security), and which is devoid of community discourse (Walby and Lippert, 2012; Lippert et al, 2013). A key purpose for exploring CSOs in Canada is to gain fresh insights into the status and possible futures of community and reassurance policing, as opposed to rival approaches such as 'intelligence-led policing' or lesser-known alternatives, which we discuss subsequently.

First, we review existing literature on CSOs in the UK and in Australia, as well as literature on criminal justice policy transfer. After a note on method, we examine CSO establishment in Canadian cities and analyse CSO practices. We conclude by conceptualising policy mutation as a distinctive, local, or regional expression of general criminal justice policy transfer. Our findings enhance understanding of CSOs and contribute to criminal justice research on reassurance and community policing, by developing insights into these mutations.

Community safety officers, policy transfer and reassurance policing

In the UK, the New Labour criminal justice policy agenda in the 1990s made a lasting impression on policing (McAra, 2008; Hodgkinson and Tilley, 2011). New forms of visible patrol and reassurance policing – including CSOs – became prevalent as a way of addressing crime concerns consistent with New Labour's criminal justice policy agenda. Reassurance policing grew most during the early 2000s to manage 'public insecurities' (Barker and Crawford, 2013: 13). Many of these forms are framed as a supplement or complement to public police (Crawford and Lister, 2004: 413), not as replacements. There are multiple reasons for this development:

- First, Crawford and Lister (2004) argue that citizens have increased demands for safety.
- Second, public police welcome load sharing that allows them to retain prominence without a duty to perform all the work.
- Third, policing in the UK has been subject to new public management that inserts performance indicators into police work, resulting in civilianisation of policing when these measures are not attained. CSOs became a strand in the new 'patchwork' of reassurance policing.

Community safety has made its mark not only in local security networks but also in academia too. New forums such as the *Community Safety Journal* and debates have emerged, which sometimes feature practitioners reflecting on CSO work. As Bailey (2003: 29) remarked, CSOs are involved in a 'dazzling variety' of practices, which describes CSOs in Canada now too.

CSOs subsequently arose in Australia. Cherney and Sutton (2004) argue that CSOs in Australia facilitate networks of local security providers. CSOs also shift the management of crime from a criminal justice model to a problem-solving approach consistent with community policing principles (Goldstein, 1990). However, Cherney and Sutton (2004) note that CSOs face funding challenges and endure at the whim of the ruling political party's position on policing. Cherney (2004) has argued that CSOs have assumed a chief role across the state of Victoria, Australia, within local safety initiatives. However, 'the short-term, contractual nature of their employment' (Cherney, 2004: 122), which is not unlike the situation of seasonal ambassadors hired sometimes at minimum wage by business improvement districts (BIDs), remains challenging.

CSOs are claimed to bring a new style and knowledge to local policing and security provision. Gilling and Hughes (2002) suggest that CSOs have professional aspirations and view themselves as significant players in local policing and security networks. The work of CSOs includes liaising with elected officials, the public, public police and the media. Hughes and Gilling (2004) argue that CSOs perceive themselves as knowledge workers and networking experts. As Shepherdson et al (2014) argue, CSOs in Australia participate in local government committees, exchanging information, participating in decision making about safety issues, and enduring what the authors call an 'administrative burden' (p. 114). CSOs are jacks of all trades.

Because of all this diversity, there is no single model of CSO work. Gilling et al (2013) have conducted comparative research on 'the uneven institutionalisation of community safety' (2013: 326) in England and Wales, as well as in Scotland, Northern Ireland and the Republic of Ireland. In England and Wales, they argue, 'institutionalization tended both to be highly dependent upon central government project funding and locally variable' (Gilling et al, 2013: 329). In Scotland, CSOs were not mandatory until 2003, which resulted in variation. Across Northern Ireland and the Republic of Ireland, CSO models vary too. Gilling et al stress that this is due to the local network aspect of community safety, which we address in relation to Canada.

Gilling (2001) has argued that community safety may be more neoliberal and exclusionary than welfarist and inclusionary. While the notion of community safety resonates well with community policing principles of prevention and partnership, and the ideas of restorative justice and dialogue, New Labour's version of community safety in the UK was to become inconsistent with the latter two concepts. From the Crime and Disorder Act 1998 onward, it included antisocial behaviour orders, which were first called community safety orders. As Gilling (2001: 398) noted, 'in the UK, community safety shows little sign of bringing about the socialization or welfarisation of criminal justice'. Hope (2005) likewise argues that the idea of community safety implies citizens and security professionals participating in a dialogue about policing issues, while most citizens have neither the time nor the social capital to do so.

These criticisms have also been lodged against the notion of community policing, of which reassurance policing and CSOs are constituents. Yet, if we focus exclusively on the deeper reality or effectiveness of CSO work, we may obscure the significance of the centrality of community discourse in CSO emergence and practices in the first place. The idea that community is a signifier in these programmes at all raises questions about community policing's future considering emergence of new policy rivals, as we discuss later.

For the RCMP in Canada, Deukmedjian and de Lint (2007: 247) note that in 1990 community policing 'appealed to the most senior levels of the RCMP' and therefore 'the Commissioner proposed the adoption of a new service-delivery mechanism for the RCMP at large'. In the 2000s, this 'problem-solving partnership between the RCMP and the "community" ... had faltered. It was displaced by a style of policing' (2007: 250) – referred to as intelligence-led policing. The idea of community policing was (and still is, we show) misaligned with the RCMP's strategic and tactical orientation. As municipal policing costs continue to increase, the role of public police like the RCMP in community policing in Canada and elsewhere remains murky, and our examination of CSOs clarifies why. The case of CSOs in Australia, and now Canada, also raises questions about criminal justice policy transfer (Jones and Newburn, 2006; Bergin, 2011).

Rather than viewing the rise of CSOs as a result of corporatism, managerialism or the offshoot of a particular political regime, we draw from literature on criminal justice policy transfer to conceptualise the establishment of CSOs in Canada. Literature on policy transfer examines how policies move across jurisdictions and how policies change. Policy transfer refers to a flow of ideas that results in policy learning. Rather than a 'cookie-cutter' application of a policy model found elsewhere, it involves adaptation of policy to local conditions. The vision of CSOs in England inspired CSOs in Canadian cities, but not in a uniform manner. Most research on policy transfer examines the national or international level, not the regional or local. The CSO model changed, not only with the initial Canadian uptake of the CSO policy idea, but also when it was transferred regionally and to other jurisdictions in Canada.

Benz and Fürst (2002) introduce the idea of policy-learning regions. They argue that regional networks in Europe are key pathways, in which policy learning can happen. Policies can move through networks quickly, even if a network is regionally distributed across a diverse country like Canada. When policies are transferred or become mobile, they often change or mutate unevenly (Peck and Theodore, 2010; Peck, 2011; Hier and Walby, 2014). Indeed, after transfer from the UK, CSOs emerged in Western Canada in regionally specific ways.

Research procedures

CSOs in the UK have been noted as an inspiration for CSOs in Canada. Simultaneously, the RCMP has introduced its own CSO model that we will show is at odds with most visions of community policing. It is thus vital to examine the rationales and funding debates for CSO justification, establishment and expansion as elements of community policing and for CSO policy diffusion among municipalities. We conducted research on community safety in Canada from 2009 to 2013. Data for this research were generated using three strategies:

- First, we located all open source material, including reports, policies and policy evaluations, as well as newspaper articles pertaining to CSOs.
- Second, where CSOs did not provide access to key documents concerning policies and policy evaluations on government websites, we submitted FOI requests to obtain them as well as CSO occurrence reports that are not usually publicly accessible. We collected approximately 400 pages of documents.
- Third, we conducted interviews with CSO personnel in three Canadian cities. Programme managers were contacted directly and asked to participate. We coded these data for excerpts pertaining to CSO work, policy and policy transfer or change. We have selected CSOs in different cities as illustrative cases, because they are indicative of trends in community policing and safety across Canada. We focus on Langford in British Columbia as being among the first municipalities to establish CSOs. We then examine Surrey, Maple Ridge and other cities in British Columbia where the RCMP created its own CSO models. The rationale for the comparative research design is to lend insight into policy transfer among municipalities as well as variations among CSOs internationally.

Langford, British Columbia: reducing the need for the RCMP

The City of Langford's CSO initiative was 'designed to employ suitably trained and equipped Municipal Bylaw Enforcement Officers as CSOs who perform an essential role and extend the range of overall activities the police are able to provide [for] the community' (City of Langford, 2007a: 5). The main policy goal was to reduce the need for the 'overstrained' RCMP to conduct municipal bylaw enforcement. Langford's was the first CSO programme in Canada.

Launched in July 2006, partially in response to citizen dissatisfaction with community safety levels, the CSO programme was designed to respond efficiently to nuisances such as graffiti and to improve public relations on streets and bicycle paths.[2] The initiative reorganised the Bylaw Enforcement Department, which was renamed Community Safety and Bylaw Enforcement, adding two officers for afternoon, evening and weekend patrol work. In Langford, CSOs were responsible for the enforcement of municipal bylaws or ordinances.

As one municipal staff member noted, at the beginning they were without a name or a plan. Officers were searching for a fitting label and vision. Eventually, Langford settled on the title of CSOs after looking into CSO arrangements in England. A local newspaper reporter remarked that CSOs 'wouldn't be armed ... and wouldn't be considered police' (Victoria Times Colonist, 2006). The CSOs had flexible schedules, permitting efficient application of resources to emerging and seasonal demands. According to a project summary, 'the immediate results were evident as congregating youth were disrupted in illicit activities and citizens quickly adopted the use of an after-hours line for immediate response by a CSO to a wide variety of community safety challenges' (City of Langford, 2009: 2). Citizen satisfaction was noted to be higher, as CSOs allowed for a quick response to issues such as graffiti and public drug use.

A problem-solving approach

The CSO programme was funded by the local council via a Provincial Traffic Fine Revenues Sharing Grant Program. Cost savings were realised from CSO bicycle patrols. The patrols reduced wear and tear on the department's fleet, thus delaying vehicle replacement needs. Bicycle patrols made the CSOs more interactive, more visible, more mobile and closer to street incidents. CSO occurrence reports obtained from FOI requests describe the number of public contacts, written warnings and verbal warnings, and the extent and nature of CSO work. Some CSOs covered 60–70km by bicycle per shift and recorded dozens of encounters with the public daily. These occurrence reports show a high volume of educative and non-enforcement interactions, including those pertaining to drug and alcohol use, bicycle road safety and personal wellbeing. Moreover, in 2009, joint bicycle patrols, consisting of one RCMP member and one CSO, were implemented to maintain patrols and to overcome summer staffing shortfalls.

A measurement tool was developed in Langford to show how programme objectives were being met. This approach produced statistics about all CSO activities for viewing by the municipal Protective Services Committee that comprises city councillors and oversees security and safety issues. Occurrence reports outlined key CSO achievements, such as a 30:1 warning to ticket ratio. CSOs had a post order for destroying drugs like marijuana, rather than ticketing or calling the RCMP. There was apparently high compliance.

This is evidence of the problem-solving approach characteristic of CSOs in the UK (Gilling and Hughes, 2002) and of community policing more generally (Brogden and Nijhar, 2005; Fielding and Innes, 2006). CSO duties included active patrol to deter illicit activity, responding to graffiti, noise and other 'antisocial' behaviours, and enforcing bylaws like the local Truck Route Bylaw to reduce street infrastructure resurfacing costs. CSOs issued municipal tickets (involving fines) for violations and appeared in court in the prosecution of disputed tickets. They patrolled in pairs on municipal property and in public spaces in marked vehicles, on bicycles and on foot, to provide a visible presence designed to heighten citizens' safety levels. The CSOs also attended evening watch briefings at the local detachment/ headquarters, to share information with the RCMP, and monitored police radio transmissions to assist as appropriate. Moreover, the CSOs were often the 'first-line' response to open fire/fire pit complaints, noisy house parties and motor vehicle accidents.

Yet the intent of the CSO initiative was to supplement – and when necessary supplant – RCMP services, by providing more visible patrols. It was argued that the programme created efficiencies in community policing, because RCMP detachments were overtasked and understaffed. Cooperation with the West Shore RCMP was part of the success of the CSO project in 2007. The RCMP viewed the 'CSOs as a significant resource for everything from on-site officer backup, traffic control at accident scenes to an alternative agency to which they can wholly discharge appropriate file work' (City of Langford, 2009: 5).

Even in Langford in 2006, the RCMP already had a police-first vision of the work of CSO personnel, suggesting that their proper role was as a support for RCMP. The CSOs sometimes worked alongside members of the RCMP or the Provincial Commercial Vehicle Safety Enforcement Inspectors as 'support officers' in joint traffic operations focusing on motoring safety. As a result, these joint assignments 'effectively served to raise the public profile of the CSOs as being part of the local public safety and enforcement landscape' (City of Langford, 2007b: 28).

Successes

As of 2007, five CSOs were operating in Langford. Their backgrounds included not only the RCMP Auxiliary Constable Program, but also the Corrections Services, Provincial Parks Operations, and the British and Australian police departments. The municipality, not the regional police, hired these personnel. They were trained in mediation, restorative justice, crime prevention through environmental design, and officer safety including self-defence training (on CSOs and crime prevention through environmental design, see Haywood et al, 2009). This training provided them with skills 'to settle disputes among neighbours, deal with "youth on the street" issues, mitigate road hazards, respond to emergencies and consult with business and home owners to lessen victimisation of themselves and their properties, through improved target hardening strategies' (City of Langford, 2007a: 5).

They relied on the federal Criminal Code's citizen arrest powers in rare cases when an arrest was required. However, Langford CSOs deferred to the police on criminal matters requiring use of force. In terms of accountability, the CSOs were subject to a complaint process like British Columbia's Police Act requirements.

CSOs worked on numerous community projects (City of Langford, 2009). For example, the Langford Council and the CSOs worked together with the local School District 62 to create policies and bylaws to help curb vandalism at Langford schools at night, by empowering the CSOs as agents for the School District on school properties. Assignment of CSOs to five 'hot' schools allegedly led to a 68% decrease in repair costs for the School District in 2007. In 2007, the CSOs also had been able to document up to 50 incidents of graffiti 'tagging' on public and private properties. This investigation allegedly resulted in location of the suspect. The file was then turned over to the RCMP and Crown

Council. The funding for two CSOs was equivalent to adding the cost of one RCMP constable to the municipality's annual budget.

A viable alternative

As Langford's was the first CSO programme in Canada, the initiative drew attention from municipal governments around the province, with more than 10 jurisdictions requesting detailed information, including Campbell River, Nanaimo, and Kelowna. The CSOs were claimed to be a viable alternative in communities without a stable, local police department.

For many in Langford, the value of the CSO initiative 'is worthy of consideration by other ... B.C. Municipalities as its design allows for an ever-widening community safety gap to be filled' (City of Langford, 2007a: 7). Furthermore, the CSO programme 'has proven itself to be an effective drive toward neighbourhood safety, with the specific aim of tackling crime, the fear of crime and ... low level social nuisances' (2007a: 3). It was also stated that: 'the CSO Initiative offers more value to a community than employing a private security service might as there are distinct Peace Officer and enforcement powers available to help maintain levels of public safety' (2007a: 7). Despite these apparent successes, the CSO programme was defunded in 2010, much to the chagrin of Langford's CSO programme leader.

The RCMP model: reassurance policing in 'E' Division

Borrowing from the Langford experience, the RCMP created a pilot CSO project to provide reassurance policing in its E Division (Surrey, Langley, Ridge Meadows, and Prince George, British Columbia). E Division is home to the RCMP's British Columbia division. Langford's CSO programme leader shared policy documents with E Division's officer responsible for the CSO pilot. The Langford manager of Community Safety and Bylaw Enforcement met with an RCMP inspector to help plan the RCMP CSO pilot. However, with the RCMP model, the goal of CSOs was to complement and become the 'eyes and ears' of RCMP officers. The purpose of the RCMP CSO pilot was 'to provide the community with additional police resources by engaging in crime prevention activities and reassurance policing' (City of Surrey, 2008a: 3).

Background

The Surrey RCMP Crime Reduction Strategy Plan for 2008 included funding for CSOs in town centres. The Plan recommended 'that the City in conjunction with the RCMP and academic researchers create a model for the role of "community safety officers" in respect to policing prevention functions in the City' (City of Surrey, 2008b: 1). The RCMP advised that they would implement the new positions on a pilot basis 'to gain knowledge about how the positions could best be utilised in the context of delivering effective police services' (2008b: 2). The CSO pilot programme was proposed to last 18 months in Surrey, Langley and Maple Ridge. The 2008 budget allowed for hiring 10 CSOs in Surrey and lesser numbers in other locations. 'It's two-tiered policing. They will be working with the community to reduce crime. The only difference is they won't be carrying guns', said Mayor Surrey Diane Watts. 'They'll deal with things like youth congregating and doing drugs, graffiti issues' (Colley, 2007: 13).

In 2008, RCMP Inspector Brett Haugli was introduced as the Surrey CSO programme manager. He stated: 'the CSOs need time to complete their training and be successful in their first assignment and the RCMP need to assess and clarify the roles and responsibilities before introducing the programme to other areas of the City' (City of Surrey, 2008c: 2). In Surrey, the 10 CSOs, who were previously RCMP auxiliary members (uniformed but unarmed members who lack full police powers), commenced training on 16 June 2008.

Unlike in Langford – and dissimilar to CSOs in relation to public police internationally (Shepherdson et al, 2014) – the RCMP themselves hired these personnel. These individuals were sent for training at the RCMP Pacific Regional Training Centre in Chilliwack and then to the Surrey RCMP detachment for orientation. After completion in August 2008, the CSOs began shifts as part of Surrey's police department. Eight of the CSOs were assigned to Cloverdale and two to South Surrey, to reach the numbers necessary to be publicly visible. The CSO role was supposed to entail observing, recording and reporting, and only limited arrests as a last resort. They also had the ability to access, open and initiate files in the RCMP database. About Surrey and Maple Ridge, another RCMP site for the CSO pilot, the RCMP were excited: "We look forward to the CSOs getting out into our community", said Inspector Jim Wakely. "They will be highly visible, and approachable, which will enhance communications, build relationships, and target local issues throughout the community" (Pitt Meadows Times, 2008: 12).

The CSOs were not subject to transfer like regular RCMP members and were recruited locally, so it was expected that CSOs could establish lasting community relationships. "We're being trained by people who have experience in our area, and so we'll be paired up with field coaches", said Constable Nenadic. "That will be a big part of orientation, getting to know the Ridge" (Pitt Meadows Times, 2008: 12). Foot patrols were planned for downtown areas, parks and school grounds, especially during summer months. The CSO uniform was like RCMP auxiliary officer dress, in consisting of the same white shirt, hats, with different patches on their sleeves and a red jacket emboldened with 'RCMP/Gendarmerie Royale du Canada Community Safety Officer'. The hope was that residents would be able to identify a CSO by their different uniform.

The CSO emphasis on visibility speaks to a certain temporal aspect of their work too. While they patrol sometimes like the RCMP, CSOs work at a pace and tempo that is different from regular RCMP patrols. CSOs are prepared to work slowly and are willing to wait to be seen, since their aim is reassurance of those who view them. (We return to this temporal aspect of the frontier in the book's conclusion.)

Role

The first CSO priority was to patrol on foot in high-traffic areas and hotspots. Their involvement was to range from road checks to special events and other high-visibility areas. CSOs also regularly dialogued with community members and business owners to aid in creating a sense of security. In Langley, CSOs welcomed all new business owners to the area and provided them with an overview of crime prevention and RCMP contact information (Langley Times, 2010: 6). CSOs also made presentations about how to deter and prevent crime and nuisance. These RCMP CSOs maintained that they are not better at local problem solving than regular officers, but can enhance RCMP officers' problem-solving ability.

To justify the project, the RCMP said that the CSO programme was based on the Police Community Support Officers (PCSOs) in the UK. "The model's the same, just consistency, communication, rapport", said CSO Steve Terrillon (Pitt Meadows Times, 2008: 12). Across the UK, the roles of PCSOs and CSOs overlap but remain distinctive, since PCSOs provide more support for crime scene investigations and front-line policing than CSOs. This contrasts with the RCMP's adoption of CSOs from Langford, which introduced a policy mutation that fully conflated these roles and the types of work they entail.

Community members and business owners responded positively. An interim Surrey CSO report stated:

> 'I have been approached by countless members of the community who have been coming up to me and saying how happy they are to see us walking around ... and when we walk in the downtown core of Cloverdale, shop owners come out and always talk with us and say on a daily basis how happy they are to see us around.' (City of Surrey, 2008b: 2)

The programme was designed to provide the RCMP with a visible presence, to build community rapport and to enhance regular officers' ability to fulfil their duties. To accomplish this, three CSOs were deployed to the Maple Ridge pilot site full time, to provide a consistent visible presence. CSO Steve Terrillon said:

> 'We are here for Maple Ridge. Regular members are going to go from department to department, or get promoted, whereas Community Safety Officers are here specifically for that purpose ... we're just enhancing. ... If you're the business owner or you're the citizen who sees the same thing over and over again that familiarity will lead to better communications between the community and the RCMP. ... So we'll be able to come back to the RCMP and say, "this is what I'm hearing on the streets, is there anything that as RCMP ... we can do?"' (Pitt Meadows Times, 2008: 12)

In these ways, the RCMP had a police-first or police-centric vision of the work of these personnel. However, the community safety notion is malleable (Edwards and Hughes, 2008; Edwards et al, 2013). The RCMP adapted the CSO idea to complement their regular duty officers. This contrasted with the Langley model, where CSOs substituted for RCMP officers, who were deemed to provide neither adequate visible patrol nor effective public liaisons. One issue that emerged is that the RCMP pilot CSOs exceeded specified duties. Appendix A of E Division's operational manual on the CSO pilot provided a list of prohibited duties, which included: arresting violators (except in exigent circumstances); being a first responder to police emergencies; providing general duty member backup; conducting traffic stops; and taking suspects' statements. Despite positive community feedback, it was noted in the RCMP's evaluation:

'There is a lack of compliance and accountability with CSO policy by some Detachment Commanders, supervisors and CSOs. Interpretation of CSO policy varied amongst the pilot sites and in a few instances, the CSO position was utilised to address detachment needs as opposed to the community's needs.' (RCMP, 2012)

This is where the disjuncture between community policing and the RCMP approach becomes evident. A CSO questionnaire revealed that 35% of RCMP CSOs had arrested someone; 59% had used items from their duty belt (primarily handcuffs); 59% had performed enforcement duties (for example issuing violation tickets, notices and orders, warnings and seatbelt checks); and 6% were physically assaulted with little or no injury. All these actions are prohibited under RCMP CSO policy.

These CSOs were also frequently deployed for criminal investigation support. The RCMP's evaluation indicated:

Use of force ... experts believe that either the CSOs need to be equipped with a pistol or they need to move to softer civilian business attire without intervention options and soft body armour ... staff advanced the position that CSOs be trained ... [to use pepper] spray, defensive baton and handcuffs. (RCMP, 2012)

The RCMP's adaptation of the CSO model was less reflective of any approach in England or in Langford and instead more closely resembled the conduct of RCMP regular duty officers. There were also questions raised about the uniform, which was not as different as had been originally proposed. The RCMP evaluation of the CSO pilot noted:

[t]he CSO uniform ... does not distinguish them from GD [General Duty] members. A member of the community may easily conclude that a CSO is a GD member upon first glance and may believe that they hold a full range of enforcement capabilities and authorities ... (RCMP, 2012)

As the RCMP evaluation indicated:

While there are potential risks associated to a CSO looking indistinguishable from a GD [General Duty] member in the public, an important factor to consider is that without a

42

recognisable uniformed presence in the community where CSOs are stationed, the final goal of the program may experience some difficulty in attaining success. (RCMP, 2012)

Therefore, CSO visibility was at times associated with regular-duty RCMP officers, contrary to the goal of providing visible patrols by officers distinct from the RCMP. The RCMP adaptation of the CSO model deviated from the one transferred to Langford. The model mutated in RCMP hands. As their evaluation noted, '[t]his deviation from the CSO program's mandate has also contributed to some overlap in activities between CSOs and some GD [General Duty] members' (RCMP, 2012). This is because the RCMP recruited persons with aspirations to work as regular duty RCMP officers and who took the opportunity to demonstrate their police prowess. (A similar 'wannabe' culture is found in private security firms in Canada, see Rigakos, 2002; in the UK, see Cooper et al, 2006.) As the RCMP evaluation suggested:

the majority of CSOs ... had plans to attempt to convert from a CSO to a GD [General Duty] member. This identifies the potential for the pilot to become a portal for individuals looking to become GD members. This career aspiration may be attributed to CSOs being Auxiliary Constables prior to assuming their new roles. (RCMP, 2012)

This finding reinforces Deukmedjian and de Lint's (2007) point about misalignment between RCMP operations and community policing. It also substantiates the claim of Gilling and Hughes (2002) that CSOs comprise a new security profession with a different skill set than public police; personnel with aspirations to be public police who were part of the CSO pilot performed roles that resembled public police, not CSOs. The auxiliary constables were a 'known and trusted' element in the RCMP stable, were recruited by the RCMP, and possessed police training and security clearance – all reasons why some had trouble in transitioning to the CSO role.[3] In 2015, the RCMP cut the programme due to several factors.

Community safety in the Province of Alberta

Gilling et al (2013: 338) note that 'urban security' is an ill-liked term in the UK and in the Republic of Ireland. In the Canadian Province of Alberta, neighbouring British Columbia, the notion of CSOs – and community safety generally – was rejected for a different moniker. Alberta municipalities have personnel whose work resembles that of CSOs. While donning uniforms that distinguish them from public police, their work in Alberta is like that of CSOs found elsewhere. However, they more often operate in rural areas and are more likely to coordinate with conservation and wildlife protection officers compared to municipal police.

In Alberta, these personnel are referred to as 'public security officers', 'public security peace officers' or 'community peace officers', all of whom have peace officer status and abide by the Public Security Peace Officer Program Policy and Procedures Manual, published by Alberta's Solicitor General. The notion of 'community' rarely appears in this manual. The variation stems from an eleventh-hour name change from community safety to public security. According to 9 November 2007 meeting minutes of the Alberta Urban Municipalities Association (AUMA) Standing Committee on Community Infrastructure, AUMA promoted the idea of a CSO programme, after examining community policing initiatives in various cities in the US, including Seattle, which had established its own version of CSOs in 2000. However, when AUMA partnered with Alberta's Solicitor General to implement the programme, the name was changed. The provincial initiative, now called the Public Security Peace Officer Program and administered by the Solicitor General, allows levels of government to obtain peace officer status for CSO-like personnel. These personnel do much the same work as their counterparts in British Columbia cities; however, in Alberta, the idea of community safety failed to resonate. Indeed, in an early iteration of the programme and draft of the policy, the notion of CSO was used.

This rejection of the moniker 'community safety', while retaining the work type, is a second major policy mutation following CSO policy transfer to Canada from the UK. This variation provides insights into the state of community policing in Canada, an issue we discuss in the conclusion. However, at least one city in Alberta – Airdrie – used the CSO notion to refer to these personnel.

CSOs in Manitoba and Saskatchewan

The CSO model has been transferred elsewhere in Canada too. In 2015, the city of Thompson, in the Province of Manitoba, implemented a CSO programme. The rationale in part was to be able to respond to a broader variety of disruptive conduct in a way that was not necessarily focused on criminalisation (Kirby, 2015). In Thompson, 24% of the city of 14,000 is Indigenous (Statistics Canada, 2012). As one programme report noted of the CSOs, 'their role is not simply to punish people behaving inappropriately in public places but also to encourage them to take steps like getting in touch with agencies that exist in order to help people with addictions and mental health issues' (Thompson Citizen, 2016). Politicians elsewhere in the province called for CSOs to be introduced in other cities and towns because of their efficacy and cost effectiveness (Braun, 2015). The Assiniboine Community College and the Province of Manitoba then launched a training programme specifically for First Nations CSOs that would bring CSOs to dozens of Indigenous communities across the province.

In the Province of Saskatchewan, North Battleford implemented a CSO programme in 2014. As was noted, '[t]he idea was to take over some of the load from the RCMP detachment so that RCMP resources can concentrate on what is described by the province as "higher impact needs," such as more serious crimes and other enforcement activity' (Cairns, 2014). Then in 2015, the government announced a programme for CSO training operated by Saskatchewan Polytechnic. A little more than six months later, CSOs were on patrol in Prince Albert (Nguyen, 2015) and elsewhere in the province. In 2017, North and South Battleford expanded their CSO programme and sang its praises (Brown, 2017). The Manitoba and Saskatchewan examples further demonstrate the pattern of CSO policy diffusion and mutation in Canada.

Conclusions

This chapter has contributed to criminological research on reassurance and community policing by examining CSOs in Western Canada. This inquiry also exemplifies the frontier theme.

- First, we have made an empirical contribution, by focusing on CSOs in an understudied region. The CSOs are operating in a realm beyond public police and in some cases act as replacements to public police in certain domains. We are once again pushing the boundaries of criminology, by considering what counts as policing and security provision.
- Second, we have made a methodological contribution, by using FOI requests and personal interviews in tandem to study CSO work and policy. Using FOI requests as a tool allows researchers to obtain internal documents that government officials produce

about their practices. This pushes the methodological boundaries of criminological work. Conceptually, we have drawn from criminal justice and criminological literatures but also from geographies of policy transfer to understand the spread of CSOs. We have identified policy mutation as a distinctive, local or regional expression of general criminal justice policy transfer, rather than a result of corporatism, managerialism or the logical offshoot of a political or economic regime (Edwards and Hughes, 2011). Here, we are again extending criminology's conceptual edges.

- Third, we have noted the intersection of CSO work and Indigenous communities and spaces in Canadian provinces. This intersection is especially prevalent in the western prairie provinces.

This research provides insights into the nature, trajectory and external influences of CSOs on urban policing in Canada. Beyond examining CSO work in Canada, we have also provided insights into international criminal justice policy transfer (Jones and Newburn, 2006) and community policing (also see Bazemore and Griffiths, 2004; Fielding and Innes, 2006; Lambert et al, 2012).

Some Canadian sites examined highlight the experience with CSOs in the UK as the impetus for creating these offices in Canada. However, every national, regional and local policing organisation's strategic orientation differs, which can lead to mutation when policies are borrowed from international or regional sites and applied locally. The first mutation did not occur with the initial Canadian uptake of the CSO policy idea in Langford; rather, policy mutation occurred as the idea was transferred within British Columbia and adopted by the RCMP. The character of this transfer is of 'emulation' in Langford and of 'inspiration' in the latter instance (Jones and Newburn, 2006: 27). McCann (2008) uses the term 'urban policy mobilities' to refer to policies that mutate when shared regionally, which aptly characterises what happened to CSOs in Canada. Policy transfer can lead to new problems when existing policy is adapted to different institutional mandates (Peck and Theodore, 2010; Peck, 2011; Hier and Walby, 2014).

In some Canadian cities, CSOs are viewed as necessary supplements or replacements for regionally based RCMP officers who cannot visibly patrol enough in urban centres. In other Canadian cities, CSOs complement the public police, although the form of RCMP CSO visibility created some confusion in these sites. In jurisdictions like Alberta, CSOs have abandoned the notion of community safety for other monikers and iterations. This second mutation in Alberta is suggestive, too, of whether public police will have a minor or a central role – and whether these arrangements retain any link to community policing and if so how.

The notion of community may not resonate in some jurisdictions, as shown in the example of Alberta. Some of what CSOs do in these municipalities, such as visible patrols, are now provided or steered in other larger Canadian municipalities by municipal corporate security units that are influenced by private sector corporate models and policy transfer from ASIS International (Walby and Lippert, 2012; Lippert et al, 2013) (Chapter Six). These corporate units operate in sharp contrast to CSOs, in that they make few overtures to 'community' and instead refer to the municipal 'corporation' as their master. In terms of visible patrols, a similar situation is the business improvement association 'ambassador' model first pioneered in US cities, and which is now found in several Canadian downtowns (Sleiman and Lippert, 2010) (Chapter Five).

The mutations in CSO policy described earlier suggest that further transfer of CSO models within Canada is not inevitable and, based specifically on the Alberta CSO-like programmes that are devoid of a community signifier, that community policing may soon be passing Western Canada by. Yet, the existence of CSOs in some British Columbia municipalities suggests that community policing, regardless of effectiveness or deeper realities, has not been displaced by intelligence-led policing or rival corporate and private sector models that eschew community discourse.

We have supplemented previous international findings on CSOs, by showing how RCMP policy makers in Canada altered an already imported policy framework to fit the strategic vision of the RCMP. The RCMP's own evaluation showed that RCMP CSOs broke the rules, substantiating the point of Deukmedjian and de Lint (2007) that community policing is misaligned with the RCMP's overall approach. CSOs are associated with a bottom-up outlook on policing and safety (Shepherdson et al, 2014), while the RCMP's adoption and adaptation of the model invert this.

Indeed, both strategic orientation within a police organisation and broader changes in policing and politics can determine how – and the extent to which – community policing policy is implemented (Murphy, 1998). The imagined direction of CSOs and its British iteration has drifted off course in Canada, lured by the red serge uniforms of the RCMP, elsewhere repelled by the softness of the community safety moniker, or sacked in the belt-tightening exercises of Canadian municipal governments.

Notes

[1]   The RCMP serves as a federal police force and contracts with numerous municipalities to provide policing services, especially in Canada's Western and Atlantic provinces.

[2]   In the early 1990s, a similar programme was explored by the resort Municipality of Whistler, British Columbia. However, at that time, it lacked the more recent confirmation by British Columbia Courts of the Peace Officer status conferred upon municipal bylaw officers.

[3]   Following the RCMP model of CSOs, the Vancouver Police Department created CSO positions in June 2013, which is another policy mutation worth examining in future research. The December 2013 British Columbia Policing and Community Safety Plan published by the Ministry of Justice also expresses interest in exploring other security delivery options beyond public police, including CSOs.

FOUR

Conservation Officers, Dispersal and Urban Frontiers

Introduction

A large body of scholarship (Eick, 2003, 2006; von Mahs, 2005; Herbert and Beckett, 2006) has revealed how socio-spatial regulation of homeless people operates in the urban core. Other writings in legal geography have focused on regulation in parks (Hermer, 1997; Mawani, 2003; Blomley, 2004; Beckett and Herbert, 2010). Public police often force homeless people away from city centres; the effects of gentrification create fewer habitable street spaces in the urban frontier (Smith, 1996) and undermine people's rights to the city (Mitchell, 2003). Yet as DeVerteuil (2006) argues, previous research has focused overly on municipal public police instead of networks of public and private agencies, and has neglected spatial regulation in peripheral urban frontiers such as alleyways, riverbanks and tree-covered ravines adjacent to urban parks. These urban frontiers are spaces where different uses of the city are possible, and conservation officers are deployed to enforce a specific version of order.

This chapter explores how National Capital Commission (NCC) conservation officers regulate homeless people in Ottawa, Canada's capital city of one million people, located several hundred kilometres north-east of Toronto, Ontario. Ottawa is one of several Canadian cities where conservation officers regulate conduct within city limits. Historically, the NCC in Ottawa had a mandate of 'beautification' through land development (Gordon, 1998; Besmier, 2003). Architects and planners took to beautifying Ottawa in the late 1890s, seeking to make its lands reflect the 'diversity' of Canada. As a 1965 NCC document put it, 'the capital of a country … becomes a symbol of nationalism and in miniature represents the spirit and life of its people' (National Capital Commission, 1965). This goal of creating a vision of Canada in Ottawa's parks is pursued by uniformed and plain-clothed NCC conservation officers. At the same time, downtown Ottawa is built on unceded Indigenous territory. The land that the NCC administers, including Parliament Hill, is the subject of an Indigenous land claim in Ontario's Superior Court (Canadian Press, 2016).

Like other capital cities, such as Washington, DC and London, UK, Ottawa's downtown area displays monuments and national symbols meant for public consumption. Capital cities are planned as ceremonial spaces (Liebowitz and Simon, 2002) ready for parades and tours, but also for shopping and weekly mass public events. As with other urban centres with tourist markets, capital cities endeavour to remove homeless people from public streets and to create an orderly aesthetic (see also Millie, 2016), in ways less subtle and oblique than those of ambassadors described in Chapter Five. Such regulation targets bodies deemed odious to tourism and the 'theme park' aesthetic (Kawash, 1998); beautification of NCC property adopts a new meaning when riddance of homeless people to achieve 'optical consistency' (Hermer, 1997: 189) becomes an unofficial mandate.

There is a twofold temporal dimension here: during the summer months, NCC officers aim to remove homeless people every morning before the parks fill with tourists; yet NCC regulation also aims to 'conserve' spaces for expressions of nationalism and to engender them with a timeless quality. Based on our research and the frequency with which 'regulars' are mentioned in the occurrence reports that we analyse later, however, the removal of homeless people from NCC land does not appear oriented towards permanent removal.

As policing agents with peace officer status under the Criminal Code of Canada, NCC officers regulate a diversity of conduct in parks, including public sex (Walby, 2009). Contributing to literature on geographies of exclusion, we focus on dispersal as the chief strategy of NCC conservation officers involved in policing homeless people. Regulations enforced by conservation officers operate to disband homeless people from consumption zones as well as spaces designed to symbolise collective and national identity in the case of NCC parks.

Existing research on conservation officers is about prevention of poaching (Pendleton, 1998; see Pendleton, 2000 on homicides). Hermer's (2002) study of how game wardens regulate a range of conduct in provincial and state parks is the exception, but unfortunately it neglects conservation officers in cities. NCC conservation officers have powers of search and seizure, but cannot make arrests without assistance of municipal, provincial or federal police. NCC officers enforce the National Capital Commission Traffic and Property Regulations, but also access Canadian Police Information Centre (CPIC) files of the individuals they stop and, in their own terms, 'intercept'. We assert that dispersal of homeless people coheres with the ambiguity of NCC land in Ottawa (NCC jurisdiction is not clear, it weaves in and out of local police jurisdiction) as well as a lack of conservation officer accountability. Dispersal powers are unofficial and stem from the ambiguity of law during enforcement rather than the specificity of the law's content.

Beyond offering an empirical study about dispersal of homeless people in one Canadian city and focusing on the work of conservation officers, our analysis supplements existing typologies of spatial regulation. Later in this chapter, we assess how dispersal policing has a specific logic that differs from the logic of banishment and more punitive forms of spatial regulation. This does not mean that we should abandon the longstanding focus on banishment and these more punitive forms in criminology; far from it. Here, we focus on 'dispersal' for three reasons:

- First, the idea of 'exclusion' is not always as precise as other terms, such as 'dispersal' and 'banishment'.
- Second, dispersal is not tantamount to reactive punishment that seeks symbolic denunciation, disciplinary 'soul training' (Shearing and Stenning, 1985), or the future-oriented correctional approach of risk management. In a more immediate manner, dispersal temporarily removes homeless people judged to lack aesthetic value.
- Third, there are several ways of conceiving of spatial regulation of homeless people, including revanchism on the 'new urban frontier' (Smith, 1996), annihilation by law (Mitchell, 1997) and banishment (Beckett and Herbert, 2010). But as DeVerteuil and colleagues (2009) have discussed, these typologies of spatial regulation focus on the punitive measures of 'state' agencies, and overly on the US. Of interest here is mining some of the nuances of spatial regulation concerning homeless people and supplementing these typologies. For reasons having to do with the specific configuration of organisations they investigated, Beckett and Herbert (2010: 6) stress that banishment 'implies a strong sense of overt state policy'. But in Ottawa we have found that regulation of homeless people is reliant on a policing network that includes private security personnel and citizen complainants, working in concert with NCC and public police agents. 'Dispersal' is focused less on a permanent removal and, in this case, we show how dispersal involves a mixed economy of public and private policing. Dispersal can also operate in conjunction with banishment; how forms of spatial regulation overlap is an empirical question. The frontier of the park, the frontier of public leisure space, is a key aspect of this, since banishment or carceral strategies cannot be enforced in a more fluid urban confluence.

In this chapter, we first discuss the idea of dispersal, with a focus on how this term supplements existing typologies of spatial regulation. We also assess the specific regulations that NCC conservation officers use in order to regulate homeless people, highlighting aesthetics as an integral element of conservation officer policing of specific spaces and times. After discussing our research method, which uses freedom of information (FOI) requests to retrieve officer occurrence reports, we detail how NCC officers: discursively position homeless people as garbage and policing work as 'cleaning'; target homeless people in Ottawa with a sense of immediacy and in particular spaces and times; and cooperate with other public and private policing agents. We conclude by returning to our threefold definition of frontier, and discussing what our analysis suggests about frontiers and policing in relation to conservation officers.

Spatial regulation on the urban frontier

Socio-legal studies of vagrancy statutes have examined how law is used to create geographies of exclusion. For instance, Chambliss (1964: 76) argued that the aim of vagrancy laws was not 'the control of laborers but rather the control of the undesirable, the criminal and the nuisance'. Foote (1956) emphasised the discretionary power of judges but also police, in criminalising homeless people through vagrancy-type laws.

Yet these classic socio-legal accounts tend to focus on policing as a form of elite-driven social regulation, placing less emphasis on aesthetics (but see Millie, 2016), spatiality and temporality than contemporary accounts. Some literature (Smith, 1996; Mitchell, 1997; Beckett and Herbert, 2010) addresses the shortcomings of classic socio-legal studies and adds an acute focus on space. DeVerteuil and colleagues (2009) have offered a critical review of this recent literature that we draw on here. Some examples of recent literature include Davis (1992) on the carceral city, the work of Smith (1996, 2001) on revanchism, and the work of Mitchell (1997) on law and the post-justice city. Here we add Beckett and Herbert's (2009, 2010) notable research on banishment. DeVerteuil and colleagues (2009) argue that this literature is crucial insofar as it focuses on how inequality and power are amplified and channelled through spatial processes. Yet DeVerteuil and colleagues (2009) offer three criticisms. They argue that:

• these works tend to focus on 'state' agencies and not enough on private agencies involved in urban security networks;

- there is an over-emphasis on punitive policing of homeless people, which may not apply to cases in different cities and countries;
- there is a tendency to focus solely on case studies in the US.

We argue that a focus on dispersal supplements typologies of spatial regulation. Dispersal can coexist with revanchist and punitive measures of regulating homeless people, but our point is that dispersal, banishment and revanchism all have specific logics concerning their approach to law, space and temporality (see Table 4.1). Our reason for focusing on dispersal is that it provides a specific concentration on non-permanent removal that reflects the character of certain forms of spatial regulation, such as what the NCC is engaged in around Ottawa. Banishment implies a community from which one is being exiled. But homeless people are typically cut off from consideration as constituents of local or higher levels of government and as possessive of a right to the city (Mitchell, 2003); they are already exiled from 'the public'. Banishment implies a permanent exclusion, where dispersal does not. Consequently, banishment may not be the best way to conceptualise some forms of spatial regulation that temporarily moves homeless people out of city spaces and does not aim for a permanent exclusion.

Table 4.1 Types of spatial regulation

Type of regulation	Role of legal knowledge	Spatial character	Temporal character
Punitive/carceral	Punishment	Fortified	Semi-permanent
Banishment	Segregation	Prohibited	Permanent
Dispersal	Removal	Mixed use	Temporary

Dispersal may coexist with banishment and other forms of spatial regulation mentioned earlier or may be the chief regulatory logic for a set of agencies. Whether dispersal or banishment or some other term is accurate is an empirical question. As a way of elaborating on what we mean by dispersal, here we answer the question: What should criminologists focus on to make sense of spatial regulation, and what are the constituent elements of spatial regulation on the frontier? Our answer is that these elements are law, aesthetics, space and temporality.

Law

Law is used differently in each form of spatial regulation. In punitive approaches, law is used to criminalise, incarcerate and punish. With banishment, law is used to permanently exclude someone from a space and community. With dispersal, we argue, law is invoked to temporarily remove a person from a space. It is important to note that vagrancy statutes (struck from the Canadian Criminal Code in 1972) associated with coercive forms of regulating homeless people have been replaced by a new set of legal knowledges, such as the Safe Streets Act (1999) in Ontario as well as parks exclusion and off-limits orders in the US (Beckett and Herbert, 2010).

The point we emphasise here regarding law and regulation of homeless people is that legal knowledges permeate other policies and guidelines, such as the NCC regulations, which become enforced as analogous to law (Valverde, 2003; Walby, 2007; Lippert and Walby, 2014). Section #38 of the National Capital Commission Traffic and Property Regulations states: 'no person shall camp, picnic or erect a tent on any property of the Commission not specifically designated by the Commission for that purpose'. No specific qualities of the 'illegal camper' are singled out with section #38 of the NCC regulations. This ambiguity in public regulations allows for highly discretionary applications. These regulations also stake out the jurisdiction of officers. Jurisdiction requires certain policing agencies to cover precise grounds (Ford, 1999); later we show that agencies like the NCC fill the jurisdictional gaps in cities.

Aesthetics

The issue of law and discretion begs the question of the basis on which discretionary practices operate. Aesthetics, we argue, are foremost. Aesthetics may inform discretion differently in spatial regulation organised according to a banishment logic compared to a dispersal logic, but we argue, as have other scholars, that aesthetics is a constant across the various forms of spatial regulation of homeless people. Blomley (2005) has usefully explored how the aesthetics of property is policed in the name of the 'public good'. Creation of a visually pleasing urban space requires sorting objects into high, low or no aesthetic value. Wakin (2008) likewise argues that anti-homeless regulation focuses on appearance as a collection of stigma symbols that signify a homeless presence. Discretionary dispersal of homeless people is also consonant with decidedly lower public visibility, as it concerns the conduct of officers. Classic accounts of policing point to low visibility for officers as that which permits discretion to be exercised unchecked (Bittner, 1967). It is on the spatial margins that this visibility is considerably less, but not zero, since the point of policing the visual order is to create and preserve an aesthetic for immediate public consumption.

Space

Banishment, dispersal and other forms of regulation have an acute spatial element. In cities with inadequate shelters, homeless persons can only sleep on private property, which is 'trespassing', or on public property, which may violate loitering ordinances and related bylaws (Amster, 2003; Williams, 2005). But not all space is produced equally. Some spaces are imbued with a notion that they must be permanently protected, so regulation that targets such threats aims for enduring exclusion. Other spaces are imbued with a notion that it is only at certain times when they must appear a specific way to users. Valverde (2005) has discussed how 'mixed use' spaces promote a proliferation of regulations, as well as times when space must be regulated.

Many of the spaces in downtown Ottawa are as such. As a capital city, Ottawa is somewhat peculiar in having numerous, highly regulated, nominally public spaces that bleed into private property. These spaces aspire to national significance (for example, parks surrounding the Parliament of Canada) and are regulated by a policing network (for example, public and private security agencies as well as municipal and provincial police). The network is also multi-scalar insofar as it draws in regulatory agencies from national levels of policing (for example, the RCMP). However, these spaces must also appear to be accessible. The officers who patrol these spaces attempt to remove homeless people, but only temporarily – and primarily when their visibility becomes a problem for tourists, business owners or residents who make complaints.

Temporality

Dispersal policing based on aesthetics is common in parks and tourist zones at specific times of day and night. Thus, spatial regulation on the frontier is not a simple matter of cartography, since temporal aspects of regulation of homeless people must remain the focus of criminologists and socio-legal scholars. We return to this point in the book's conclusion.

Analysis of legal 'technicalities' – such as jurisdiction – alerts social scientists to where legal governance happens in the city, but a focus on temporality demonstrates how agencies can operate with two or more operational goals, some of which can be future oriented (for example, risk management), whereas others can focus on past conduct (for example, retribution) (Valverde, 2009). The lands to which homeless people retreat, as well as the character of NCC policing, differ at night and in the early morning hours, suggesting that criminology should account for the spatialities and the temporalities of regulation.

Research procedures

Responding to calls for detailed empirical case studies of the regulation of homeless people outside the US (von Mahs, 2005; DeVerteuil et al, 2009), our research focuses on the unique role that conservation officers play in governing parks and adjacent spaces in a major Canadian city: Ottawa.

One tool that conservation officers use is the occurrence report. Containing columns for recording infraction details and Canadian Police Information Centre code, these reports allow for activity to be described in actionable terms and shared with other conservation officers and policing agencies. We have used FOI requests to collect the occurrence reports of NCC conservation officers. In the tradition of Marx's (1984) comments on 'dirty data', these requests allow researchers to explore beneath analyses of official texts of policing agencies, to examine more closely officers' discourses and practices.

Relying on official texts to the neglect of 'lower-level' texts authored and used by those who engage in governing practices has been called into question (for example, Park and Lippert, 2008; Walby and Monaghan, 2010). Valverde (2003) argues that rather than discussing 'the law' generally, it is more fruitful to empirically investigate techniques of regulation. Pushing the methodological frontiers of criminology, FOI can help to illuminate details of these techniques, which otherwise would rarely come to light.

We requested NCC reports, communications and/or briefing materials regarding homelessness and 'illegal camping' in NCC parks. We received 530 occurrence reports from 1998 to 2009 and other documents related to policing homeless people (for example, notes between officers). Some retrieved documents contained personal information redacted consistent with section 19(1) of the National Capital Commission Traffic and Property Regulations. We also accessed complaints by storeowners and users of park trails concerning homeless people. We analysed NCC occurrence reports to detail officers' justifications for ticket distribution, with concern for the spatialities and temporalities of NCC officer dispersal. Reflective of the limits of FOI research, we have not been able to collect data on how many occurrences these 530 occurrence reports from 1998 to 2009 represent in the total number of NCC occurrence reports produced over the decade, as asking for all occurrence reports would be too costly. Nor does the NCC make such figures publicly available.

We are unable to supplement our analysis of these occurrence reports through interviews with NCC conservation officers, because at no point during this research (before or after the submission of the FOI requests) did the organisation allow its officers to speak with us about their work. However, at one point, the first author did discuss the possibility of interviews with the lead conservation officer, who stated: "I am not sure what else we can tell you … the occurrence reports pretty much sum up our approach to things".

We are also not exploring the broader welfare apparatus in Ottawa, which, despite deep funding cuts, coupled with movement of responsibility for welfare from provincial to municipal levels of government in the mid-1990s in Ontario (Chunn and Gavigan, 2004), can be less austere than the actions of policing agents (DeVerteuil, 2006). Instead, our empirically grounded study attempts to understand the complexity of dispersal policing in one milieu.

Dispersal policing of homeless people: cracking down on the 'illegal camper'

Ottawa is a city of one million people, in which shelters and outreach services for homeless people are chronically underfunded (Klodawsky et al, 2002). Inattention to the issue of homelessness by the City of Ottawa came to a head in the spring of 2007, when Mayor Larry O'Brien referred to panhandlers (a Canadian and US term for people begging for money on street corners) as pigeons, suggesting that if the City stopped feeding them, they might just go away.

This 'get "them" to go away' approach to homelessness has been amplified by major architectural projects in Ottawa's downtown that consumed public lands, for example the completion of the National Gallery of Canada in 1988 and the American Embassy in 1999. These have led to intensive management of the images produced in urban space, and the NCC is closely involved. NCC conservation officers use section #38 of the NCC regulations concerning 'illegal camping' as a resource to expel homeless people, whose principle 'wrongdoing' is sleeping or preparing an area to sleep. 'Illegal camping' is the most common ticket, typically issued by officers on foot or bike patrols. Even when a ticket is not distributed, dispersal remains the goal.

For instance, on 1 June 2003, a conservation officer on a path in Major's Hill Park 'observed one of our regulars sleeping in the flower beds. Couldn't wake him up. Had Ottawa Police Service [OPS] come and assist. Fire department came by too. We had to use a pole to wake him up. Expelled.' The NCC 'illegal camping' regulation is not an anti-sleeping ordinance, but is used that way. The idea that NCC officers can recognise and name their 'regulars' suggests that this homeless man had been caught on NCC land before and would be again, hence our emphasis on temporary dispersal (to be discussed later).

Occurrence reports offer no rationale for why certain bodies are targeted or actions taken. For example, on 10 June 2002, an officer 'observed [a] homeless man sleeping on the ground, OPS took him.' Frequently no justification is offered for NCC officer 'interceptions' other than the sight of a homeless person. For instance, on 27 May 2004, one officer 'observed a white male person stretched on a bench' who was subsequently 'expelled (because he was not normal)'.

These examples show the lengths to which NCC officers go to prevent homeless people from sleeping and being seen during certain hours on NCC lands, but also reveal how officers must 'stretch' conduct to justify regulation. The man lying on the bench must be described as 'not normal', since laying on a bench itself cannot be construed as 'illegal camping'.

NCC officers are often assigned tasks in response to public complaints, primarily from residents of neighbourhoods that border NCC parks or from other policing agencies and businesses. For instance, on 26 September 1999, an officer 'observed clothing, personal stuff, lighter, camping equipment, and one towel full of defecation ... dear night shift, catch the camper! Denis, you can do it!!!! 3 complaints in three days.' In another instance, on 31 May 1999, there is a 'call from [a] business about 2 squeegees camping, expelled'. On 29 August 2003, the NCC received a 'call from kayaker about vagrant making himself a shelter in bushes behind TransCanada monument ... lots of garbage (mattress, chair, stool)'. Use of the label 'vagrant' by NCC officers has emerged informally, and with it the derogatory label 'squeegees', meant to refer to homeless young people who wash car windows for change.

'Illegal camper' is a more innocuous and, we suggest, insidious term. The deployment of the legally defined 'camper' in occurrence reports is significant, since it denies the reality of homelessness: only someone with a permanent private dwelling 'camps' elsewhere. Camping is leisure, not born of necessity. Its association with leisure rather than survival obscures the gravity of homelessness. Use of these quasi-legal labels such as 'illegal camping' allows regulations to be applied to bodies that are, by that very fact, disqualified from public space.

Beckett and Herbert (2010) usefully demonstrate how new regulations in the city, such as some trespass admonishments, do not require officers to provide a written justification for expulsion, and the case is similar with NCC officers. For instance, on 25 June 1999, an officer 'observed one vagrant sitting down in York court yard, after arguing for 10-15 minutes he wouldn't move, called OCRP [Ottawa Carleton Regional Police, which became the OPS in 2001], Officer Love came along and removed it.' The person is posited as a mere object in this report. Exactly why sitting in a courtyard at midday is a problem is not explained.

On 21 April 2001, an NCC officer 'intercepts an individual gathering garbage bags to make a shelter'. The individual was expelled. While gathering garbage bags is plainly inadequate to justify an 'intervention', this is often the only kind of justification provided. The ambiguity of public order regulations such as the NCC's allows ubiquitous application, but simultaneously forces officers to 'stretch' the conduct of homeless people to initiate a so-called 'interception'. Enforcement of the 'illegal camping' regulation is one example of the 'inevitable divide between legal form and legal content' (Valverde, 2008: 921).

These reports raise questions about how NCC officers discursively position homeless people and rationalise their own work, especially regarding 'interceptions' that are highly discretionary. For instance, at 6:10 am on 15 May 2008, one officer writes that he 'intercepted' two individuals sleeping, woke them up, advised them of the regulations, ticketed and expelled them. At 6:10 am on 22 May 2008, one officer writes that he 'intercepted and woke up' someone sleeping behind the heating plant. The language of 'interception' is constant across our sample of occurrence reports, which suggests an organisational logic of dispersal.

Aesthetics – or cleaning up the frontier

The only publicly available map of NCC parks is part of the NCC's preferred aesthetic, especially the orderly green spaces and sanitised corridors that complement Ottawa's buildings of national import. Like the ambassadors we examine in Chapter Five, conservation officers are asked to enforce park regulations that envision clean and safe parks in Canada's capital – clean and safe urban frontiers that are devoid of the inequalities and conflict that major cities generate.

Consistent with the growing socio-legal literature on aesthetics and urban order (Hermer, 1997; Mitchell and Staeheli, 2006; Ghertner, 2010), NCC conservation officers often approach homeless people as garbage and do not distinguish between homeless people and their belongings as objects for removal from parks. This is evident in NCC officer occurrence reports, which describe the work of dispersal as 'cleaning'.

On 28 August 1999, NCC officers reported that 'vagrants have been sleeping under the King Edward Bridge, lots of cushions, clothes, tarps and towels, to be removed and cleaned'. On 2 April 2003, a conservation officer 'observed [a] shelter along pathway, needs to be cleaned'. This NCC officer sketched a map to the shelter's location, so it could be removed. Like the photographs discussed later, this map sketched by the officer is less of a representation and more an 'inscription device' (Blomley and Sommers, 1999: 265) that makes reality 'stable' and 'comparable' (Rose and Miller, 1992: 185) for other regulatory personnel.

The creation of sanitised spaces appears to be the goal of dispersal policing. For instance, on 7 July 1999, there was a 'report from Terra Pro [a local gardening company] of vagrant belongings in the bush, all garbage, destroyed'. On 18 September 2002, there was a complaint about 'two males camping on Maple Island, observed both males, woke up, issued tickets for illegal camping. Suspects uncooperative. Had them remove 2 red mattresses ... site still needs to be cleaned up.' And on 19 September 2000:

> ... complaints about vagrants sleeping at Queen Street across from World Exchange Plaza. The area is a slum. It smells of urine. This is a major health issue. Area needs to be cleaned up and also needs to be secured with some type of cage to close off the area to the vagrants, trees in the corner of the parking lot could also be removed so they have no place to hide or shelter themselves.

In this excerpt, public health problems are conflated with, and blamed on, homeless people. 'Cleaning' in this sense refers to dispersal as the primary strategy of NCC officer work. NCC officers also force homeless people to 'clean up' their living quarters before being dispersed from the site. One man living in a makeshift home in a ravine is 'intercepted' by NCC conservation officers and ticketed under section #38, after a complaint from a resident of Ottawa's Hemlock area. The man is required to clean up the site in two days, during which NCC conservation officers periodically return to monitor his progress. On the second day, they 'waited approximately 30 minutes until the suspect was finished with the clean up', before expelling him. On 22 August

2001, an NCC officer observes a man on NCC land 'using the place for permanent habitat … we told him he had until 2100h to clean the place and leave'.

If one NCC goal remains making Ottawa a visible 'symbol of nationalism', to represent the spirit and life of Canada in miniature, this is a picture in which homeless people are not so much touched up or painted over, as briefly enlisted in the artistry and then forcibly marched out of the frame.

Policing through aesthetics is consonant with the 'broken windows' thesis, inspired by a 'safe and clean' project in Newark, New Jersey (Wilson and Kelling, 1982). 'Broken windows' policing seeks to remove alleged visible signs of disorder from a location, including things but also persons treated as things that are imagined to invite more chaos and crime in the vicinity. There is a palpable immediacy promoted in 'safe and clean' programmes as they spread to North American urban cores (Lippert, 2007: 31), since disorder is thought to rapidly result from visible 'broken windows' that remain. The broken windows thesis has been applied throughout North America; Wilson and Kelling (1982: 31) identify the 'unchecked panhandler' as 'the first broken window'.

Yet this thesis has always directed attention to regulating streets, rather than to parks and peripheral spaces (for example, riverbanks or ravines). Of greater relevance for our case is the NCC mandate for 'beautification' of parks. The belongings of homeless people are characterised as contrary to the 'beautification' mandate. For instance, on 30 May 2008, officers come across what they describe as 'a "mini village" with lots of debris' on Colonel By Drive near Heron Road Bridge. In addition to section #38, the man was issued with a written warning under section #25 of the NCC Regulations, which states 'no person shall throw, deposit or leave any refuse or debris on property of the Commission other than in such places as are specifically designated for that purpose'. He is forced to clean up the site within 72 hours. On 26 April 2004, two NCC officers arrive at Major's Hill Park after a complaint to find blankets, which they 'disposed of in the garbage'. NCC officers refer to the belongings of homeless people as 'garbage'. On 10 May 2004 a man is forced to 'remove the garbage' and 'remove his shelter' after being 'intercepted'. On 18 May 1999, an officer writes that 'vagrants and shelter to be cleaned-up'.

NCC officers are also summoned by municipal police to 'clean' when homeless people are dispersed by another agency unavailable to do it: on 29 June 2002, the NCC receives a 'report from City of Ottawa, police expelled a bunch of vagrants, they left a large mess behind.

Would need to be cleaned up ASAP.' Conservation of the aesthetic requires immediate action, 'as soon as possible', now.

NCC conservation officers often 'intercept' homeless people who are asleep or who exhibit visible signs of homelessness, thus further flagging the link between aesthetics and discretion. As well, sometimes NCC conservation officers will photograph what they encounter – often makeshift homes in wooded areas – as though they are crime scenes. For example, on 29 June 2008, one officer wrote: 'observed one male sleeping under bridge with pillow and sleeping bag ... woke up, took picture, written warning advised four weeks ago so issued ticket at 38, then expelled'.

On 22 May 2008, conservation officers observe 'a shelter made out of cardboard, tarps, inside shelter a sofa'. The person living here was 'intercepted' and ticketed for 'camping'. Officers then referred others to the photographs of this shelter. These photographs construct reality and are distributed to other policing agencies. The fact that the pictures are referenced in occurrence reports (for example, 'took picture') means they are an accepted practice that appears – from comments on the back of reports – to highlight 'optical inconsistencies' in the overriding aesthetic for the next shift of officers. Such photographs permit NCC officers to visually represent what they deem to be inconsistent with the imagined aesthetic in difficult-to-access outdoor sites. This visual technology is easily transferred to other officers for tactical interventions, but also to NCC bureaucrats (to train new NCC officers).

The focus on aesthetics is evident in the types of conduct that the NCC conservation officers problematise and how they do it. The language of NCC regulation #38 – that 'no person shall camp, picnic or erect a tent on any property of the Commission not specifically designated for that purpose'– aspires to the universality of law (Valverde, 2003). Yet the regulation is enforced unequally; only unsightly bodies are dispelled from specific spaces, disqualifying them from urban existence. These bodies are frequently visibly stationary, as well as without a home, and therefore, in the words of one NCC officer, 'not normal'.

The foregoing thus also suggests that in urban parks, as much as on sidewalks with 'loiterers' (Hermer, 1997), urban law in its myriad forms dreams of a near constant flow of people through spaces to produce or to consume, before they return to private property. Those deemed to do neither, and to be without a place of return, become inconsistent with this relentless moving picture. They become a target, to be intercepted and moved out of the way by a public-private policing network that includes conservation officers.

Dispersal and the resource of law

Urban parks and peripheral spaces – such as along riverbanks, in ravines, all the spots sought out by homeless people in evading municipal police – are increasingly subject to the gaze of policing agencies. In this regard, NCC officers are preoccupied with ensuring that homeless people are not present on NCC land.

This spatialisation of law enacts particular forms of space to prohibit certain kinds of conduct (Blomley, 2003). Precise spaces are targeted: bluffs, bushes, under bridges, anywhere homeless people can seek refuge. For example, on 7 June 2001, 'George showed me [an officer] a good place for a vagrant, a sleeping bag was at that place, I checked all my shift but nobody was there'. On 7 May 1999, NCC officers are 'looking round for 3 homeless close to Pretoria Bridge … we never found after three times'. On 13 June 1999, complaining about his inability to expel a homeless person from Ottawa, one conservation officer writes: 'not a new vagrant. Keeps promising to go out west … still waiting'.

Certain spaces become problematised as 'hotspots', for instance the York Street courtyard in downtown Ottawa, which is popular among tourists but is in close proximity to several soup kitchens. When complaints are received about these areas, occurrence reports sometimes call 'conservation officers for action'. Similarly, on 12 June 2004, one officer writes to the others that 'a conservation officer should return at night' to a location where he observed a blanket near Nepean Point. On 4 May 2001, an officer writes that Major Hill's Park, another popular tourist area, has become: 'a major problem area. It will just keep getting bigger.'

Preventing the sight of homeless people appears to be a central task of NCC officers. On 31 July 1999, there is a 'report from (exempted, 19.1) about four male vagrants sleeping in the courtyard. She said she wanted them moved, didn't look good for the tourists.' As this report suggests, the blitzes are prompted by complaints from private business owners. A 'blitz' mentality of policing homeless people also appears in some NCC reports. Occurring in Canada's capital city for some time, these sweeps are in part led by NCC conservation officers (Klodawsky et al, 2002). On 10 June 2004, one NCC officer writes that he observes seven people sleeping in Major's Hill Park and he moved in to 'ship them out'. On 17 May 2004, the OPS contacts the NCC to step up patrols near the York Street courtyard. The OPS officer tells the NCC officer that they 'go to that location 5 to 6 times per day and charge the street kids who are sitting on the steps with trespassing'.

However, the spatialisation of law is bolstered by the temporal dimensions of policing, which aim for restoration of 'optical consistency'. The timing of 'interceptions' – and the persistent concentration on those merely seeking to sleep – reveals the temporal aspect of NCC officer dispersal strategies. The occurrence reports reveal that interventions tend to occur at night or during early morning hours, when sleep is sought. The issue of compassion also becomes key, since homeless people are at times in need of medical care; dispersing them from the site can exacerbate their health problems. For example, on 4 August 2003, 6:30 am, an officer:

> observed a young couple camping beneath Alexandria Bridge. Both male and female were sick. The couple advised me the female may be pregnant, I advised them to immediately go to a clinic and be verified by a doctor. They advised me they were going at 8 am ... expelled.

Moving people out of the frame remains the goal, even when homeless people face peril. For instance, on 6 June 1999, one conservation officer writes that he 'observed new vagrant in possession of Listerine, he informed me he was going to drink it on the bench ... stared at him until he left'.

It is often noted in the policing literature that much policing work entails community service; policing agents sometimes wear social worker hats (see Huey, 2007). NCC officer policing and its immediacy is not organised around a concern for the wellbeing of people they encounter, although several occurrence reports mention that officers have taken homeless people to nearby shelters. This approach to poverty management (DeVerteuil et al, 2009) does not aim to secure prosecution as in punitive strategies. Instead, the strategy is dispersal from the present.

Policing networks and the frontier as contested urban space

As DeVerteuil and colleagues (2009) note, typologies of spatial regulation tend to focus overly on 'state' agencies. NCC officers are just one node of an urban public-private policing network that regulates homeless people in Ottawa. NCC conservation officers coordinate with municipal police, the RCMP and, central to our argument, private security firms.

The officers note what actions to take concerning homeless people they detect, as this example from 6 May 2008 demonstrates: '[R]eceived a call concerning a homeless man sleeping on a bench at Major's Hill Park, security guards called it in. Advised them that they could expel him or that tomorrow morning we will.' On 20 May 1999, an officer 'observed one vagrant sleeping on the bench, when vagrant got up he fell and got up and fell again … called the OCRP, vagrant began crying spontaneously a few times, OCRP left with vagrant'. Or on 26 June 1999: '[S]leeping vagrants, could not wake up. Contacted OCRP, dragged one to car and escorted to cells.'

Thus, when dispersal fails, this network of agencies will pursue punitive measures. When an arrest is deemed necessary, NCC conservation officers typically call federal (RCMP) or municipal (OPS) police. For instance, on 3 August 2003, an officer 'observed one individual sleeping with blankets … called RCMP. Advised it would take 10 minutes. The guy left. Cancelled the RCMP.' On 25 May 2004, an individual found on NCC property 'got caught by OPS and is now out of the way'. There is no description other than 'camping'. On 27 June 2003, an officer 'observed a vagrant sleeping on NCC ground … intercepted, not cooperative, called OPS for assistance, expelled by OPS'. The efforts of various police agencies overlap with those of NCC officers in the regulation of Ottawa's homeless people.

Private security agents are intimately involved in regulating homeless people in Ottawa. On 5 July 2002, there is a 'call from Securitas about illegal camping at Stanley Park, on scene at 830am, 2 people under a blue tarp, expelled'. Securitas, a transnational security firm that has captured a large segment of the private security market in Ottawa, detects homeless people on various properties around the city and alerts external agencies to assign an enforcement officer. On 8 June 2002, there was a 'report from Securitas about a vagrant under Sapper's bridge'.

These reports indicate widespread knowledge sharing between public and private policing agencies. Beyond private security, other key agents are drawn into the network. On 5 July 2003, 7:55 am, there is a 'call on emergency line from Parks Canada, lots of streets kids (20+) camping under Plaza bridge, woke everybody up and told them to pack-up …'. On 20 July 2003, the NCC 'received a call from the National Art Gallery security guard regarding camping and making a fire on NCC property, intercepted, served them each with a ticket for camping'. On 26 April 2003, the NCC received a 'call from maintenance crew through dispatch, some people camping on park property ... arrived on site ... welfare people!'

The NCC makes complaints to other agencies when it is overextended or when it would be simpler for security agents to intervene. For example, on 3 June 1999, an NCC officer 'called Museum security to expel vagrants'. This public–private policing network (Wood and Shearing, 2006: 27) manifests itself in the sheer number of agencies enlisted to work together.

Since NCC work is sometimes about responding to this information from other parts of the network or to public complaints, it reveals their varied pace and tempo too. Sometimes, NCC officers are engaged in regular patrols or quick 'blitzes' of NCC spaces far from regular paths where homeless people are living or other transgressors are situated. At other times, NCC personnel wait and watch in the shadows of the identified spaces about which they have received a call or complaint, to observe the infraction and literarily see who 'comes out of the bush'. Their pace and tempo differ from other new and neglected agents discussed in other chapters and to some degree from regular public police work too. We return to this subtheme of temporality of frontiers in the conclusion of the book.

Beyond demonstrating that those regulating homeless people in Ottawa are not limited to state agencies, these examples indicate that designating jurisdiction in policing networks is difficult. Governing agents must ask 'whose property is this' to ensure they are operating in their jurisdiction. Property discourse implies a sense of who belongs in some space and who does not (Blomley, 2004; Valverde, 2005). NCC officers, only mandated to work on NCC parklands, need to ensure a given property is theirs before 'intercepting' problematic conduct, but we have found that they tend to ignore these designations of jurisdiction. On 29 July 2002, one conservation officer 'observed a tent just North of the Queensway and south of Hampton Park, called to confirm if NCC property, he was 99% sure, issued two tickets'. On 16 June 1999, a conservation officer writes that one homeless man 'claims portion of the courtyard he is sleeping on is not NCC property, it is possible ... expelled'.

Jurisdiction matters for how urban spaces are targeted, but there are other examples of NCC conservation officers exceeding their official mandate of 'conservation', by engaging in order maintenance policing and acting outside their jurisdiction. On 6 July 2004, NCC officers 'observed a street kid holding a sign asking for money ... intercepted'.

On 19 April 1999, an NCC officer observes 'one squeegee asking for money, wiping windows … checked CPIC'.

The NCC is peculiar, because its agents have their own regulations to enforce on NCC lands. Yet, they are enlisted in a public-private network, when they coordinate 'blitzes' so that conservation officer policing at once spills out of NCC jurisdiction across the topography of problematised conduct in Ottawa. We suggest that analysis of spatial regulation must also account for temporalities, since regulation does not only trickle down from cartographical designations (maps). The occurrence reports reveal that NCC officers cooperate – rather than compete – with private security agencies to form a public-private network.

Conservation officers continue to work on the frontiers of policing. In 2016, a junior conservation officer working for the NCC shut down a kids' lemonade stand, because they lacked a permit and it was set up in an NCC park across the street from their home (Brown, 2016). The officer was enforcing the NCC land use regulation. In 2016, the NCC made it very difficult for an Indigenous woman to honour her murdered daughter and hold a vigil for missing and murdered women at Victoria Island on the Ottawa River. The woman accused the NCC of blocking entrance to the site with large snow mounds, which prevented access of other Indigenous people who planned to visit to participate in the vigil and protest (Bay, 2016).

These are examples of NCC conservation officers governing space and conduct. Relatedly, reflecting on a 30-year career, in 2015 a retired conservation officer on the other side of the country in Kelowna, British Columbia, complained about the great number of laws that conservation officers were being asked to enforce and the amount of conduct that conservation officers were being asked to regulate (Helston, 2015). Their mission was deemed to be becoming more and more like public policing. Notably, conservation officers in British Columbia underwent combat training in 2016 and had begun wearing bulletproof vests in 2014 (Mackin, 2016). The expanding powers and scope of conservation officer policing is further evidence of their work on the frontiers of policing.

Beyond our empirical contribution concerning conservation officers' regulation of homeless people, we have supplemented typologies of spatial regulation. We have differentiated dispersal from banishment, to argue that dispersal policing has several distinguishable spatial and temporal characteristics. Dispersal and banishment can coexist as logics for organising spatial regulation in some cities and among some agencies, although with our case study the eternal return of 'regulars' for NCC conservation officers indicates that the goal is not a permanent banishment from NCC lands.

While the forms of banishment that Beckett and Herbert (2009) investigated are closely linked to state policy, and NCC officers are certainly state agents, dispersal policing in our case depends on a network involving private agents. Moreover, as a form of spatial regulation, dispersal, unlike banishment, is largely hidden from view in Ottawa and not intended to convey denunciatory messages about living on NCC land or related 'transgressions' to an onlooking public. Banishment also implies a community from which one is banished, but other scholars (for example, Mitchell, 1997) contend that regulation of homeless people is possible primarily because they are already expelled from 'the public'.

Conclusions

This chapter has examined NCC conservation officers' policing of homeless people in Ottawa. Our findings reflect the threefold definition of frontier from the introduction.

First, the idea of frontier is seen here in policing work beyond traditional tasks undertaken by public police. Conservation officers, and the policing work that they do, have not been fully investigated by social scientists. We have focused on the occurrence reports of conservation officers, as a means of understanding how dispersal policing involves law, aesthetics, space and specific temporalities. These reports shed light on the broader pattern of 'interceptions' and the NCC's hidden orientation towards homeless people. Research in the US has found that conservation officers now coordinate with Homeland Security (Carter and Gore, 2013). These conservation officers collect information and share it with intelligence fusion centres, operating as new eyes and ears in the US war on terror as well.

Second, the idea of frontier can refer to the way scholars take up an analysis of policing by cutting across traditional disciplinary or methodological boundaries. In terms of disciplinary and conceptual work, we have drawn from critical geography but also from socio-legal studies as well as criminology and criminal justice studies. All conceptual resources that these disciplines bring to the table are needed to investigate new forms of policing and security practices such as conservation officer work. In terms of methodological contributions, this chapter shows how powerful FOI requests can be, by revealing organisational practices of social control and government agencies. Moreover, the focus on occurrence reports is novel and revealing of patterns in conservation officer policing. These patterns would not otherwise be illuminated, highlighting the importance of FOI research for future inquiries in criminology and socio-legal studies. We suggest that similar patterns may be discovered using these methods in the urban frontiers of other capital cities, such as London, Belfast, Washington and Canberra among others, with each requiring empirical research.

Third, the idea of frontier as we use it in this book also intersects with anti-colonial analyses or how old and new forms of policing reinforce colonial power structures. As some examples in this chapter demonstrate, NCC conservation officers are involved in policing Indigenous persons at times – and in ways – that may lead to criminalisation of Indigenous persons and extension of these colonial relations. Moreover, from a critical colonial perspective, NCC control of Ottawa lands represents an occupation of contested, unceded Indigenous territory. What this means is that Indigenous people, specifically the Algonquin First Nation, never ceded through treaty the land that now comprises NCC jurisdiction. The Algonquin First Nation have, in fact, filed a land claim in Ontario's Superior Court to take the land back (Canadian Press, 2016) from the NCC and the federal government. There is a sense in which the dispersal of Indigenous people in the account in this chapter mirrors and reproduces how these people were dispersed from their own lands on the frontier, and forced into reserves, far from the new urban environs being built on these lands, where they would not be seen by non-Indigenous people.

As with other forms of policing, accountability and oversight for conservation officer work is sorely lacking. Bittner (1967) long ago pointed to the lack of oversight of peace officer enforcement. Our analysis suggests that this absence of accountability is rooted less in the peace officer designation and more in the urban spaces that conservation officers at once regulate and produce through dispersal strategies as elements of local and national imaginings of Canada's capital city. Murphy (2009) argues that dispersal as a form of spatial regulation creates spectral geographies that hide homeless lives from view. The near invisibility of the nooks and crannies of these parks and lands on the frontier – especially at night and in the early morning hours – that attracts homeless people ensures that NCC dispersal policing remains largely sight unseen.

FIVE

Ambassadors on City Centre Frontiers

Introduction

Roving teams of brightly uniformed 'ambassadors' increasingly patrol the city centre frontiers of western cities as diverse and far-flung as San Diego (US), Nottingham (UK) and Winnipeg (Canada). According to one Canadian programme, ambassadors' prime directive is to 'welcome everyone' to the city centre. Upon closer study, however, ambassadors are engaged in both more and less than this mantra suggests.

Ambassadors do more than this, by seeking to secure the frontier of urban consumption zones through an array of direct, oblique and occasionally unofficial strategies. Prohibited from acting or self-representing as public police or private security, occasionally ambassadors flirt with such appearances or feign direct communication with these authorities to their own advantage. These efforts are intended to encourage panhandlers/beggars, 'loitering' youths, homeless people and other street 'nuisances' to cease their conduct or to move on.

Thus, ambassadors also do less than 'welcome everyone' to the city core. Not unlike diplomats of dominant nations engaging less powerful ones, downtown ambassadors are, ultimately, backed up by coercive force, should their polite cajoling and visibility fail to deter undesirable conduct or spark a hostile reaction.

While typically initiated, financed and managed by downtown business improvement districts (BIDs) (sometimes called business improvement areas or associations) or similar entrepreneurial organisations devoted to urban revitalisation, ambassadors also require tacit cooperation from public police, who (still) possess coercive capacities and whose traditional territory they now patrol. How ambassadors relate to public police is therefore paramount to the 'clean and safe' security that ambassadors seek to provide and embody on city centre frontiers. This chapter focuses on these aspects.

Ambassador patrols

Ambassador programmes have appeared across North America in recent years, and their numbers continue to expand. The ambassador concept was developed in the US and transferred to Winnipeg and Vancouver, and later to the UK and beyond. There are currently at least 14 Canadian programmes operating in downtown BIDs, including in Winnipeg, Vancouver, Kamloops, Sudbury, Moncton and Thunder Bay. In the US, ambassadors have been operating for several years longer in even more cities (at least 31), including Cleveland, Baltimore, Philadelphia, San Diego, Boston, San Antonio, Seattle, Atlanta, Austin, Portland, Minneapolis, Santa Monica, Dayton, Nashville, Denver, Charlottesville, Milwaukee, Phoenix, Honolulu, Jacksonville, Cincinnati, New Haven and Berkeley. More recently, ambassadors have come to Detroit, Colorado Springs, El Paso, Reno, Lexington and Little Rock, and are in smaller US cities like East Lansing, Michigan and Huntington Beach (California) too. Among the first ambassador programmes in the UK was in Sheffield in the late 2000s and they have since proliferated. Ambassadors are found in at least 9 UK cities: Liverpool, Brighton, Manchester, Nottingham, Chester, Cardiff, Oxford, Cambridge and Belfast, among other city centres.

Due to mutations that occur when policing and security programmes are transferred to other countries (as with community safety officers migrating from the UK to Canada described in Chapter Three), these UK programmes have not explicitly adopted the 'clean and safe' mantra. Nonetheless, as in North America, they seek to report 'antisocial behaviour' (Millie, 2008) or similar nuisance, to serve as 'eyes and ears' surveillance for police, or both. These ambassador programmes are all associated with, or overseen by, a city centre BID. In some Canadian and UK cities, ambassador patrols tend to be small, sometimes only two or three patrols at any given time, whereas in large US cities like Detroit, Baltimore and Minneapolis there are often many more ambassadors on patrol.

BIDs themselves are legally defined organisations, administered by a board that manages funds produced by a mandatory levy on all commercial property owners in a downtown area or other major retail strip (Hoyt, 2003; Lippert, 2007, 2010), which provides monies for physical security for that area. Whereas BIDs are emergent in the UK (Ward, 2007; Cook and Ward, 2012), continental Europe (Peyroux et al, 2012) and South Africa (Miraftab, 2007), in North America their establishment within urban revitalisation projects is now a given (compare Marquadt and Füller, 2012).

A key question for ambassadors, as for many other security agents discussed in this book, is whether and how they 'link' with the public police. Ambassadors rely on tacit public police cooperation. Ambassadors are often equipped with training from the police about how to transfer knowledge created from observing crime scenes into preferred police formats too. Such training is to aid ambassadors in avoiding detection and in ensuring a reliable flow of information to the public police.

Previous accounts of security provision in BIDs from the policing and security literature (for example Vindevogel, 2005) tend to neglect crucial spatial aspects of 'clean and safe' efforts exemplified when BIDs seek to increase pedestrian traffic mostly on public sidewalks to facilitate consumption. Correspondingly, 'clean and safe' security modes such as ambassador programmes, which may appear to be wholly private endeavours on the surface, are 'anchored' by public police. They point to the need to acknowledge logics, contingencies and reflexivity in relation to BID governance and security provision on this frontier.

Governing logics and security

This chapter investigates ambassador programmes from a sociology of governance perspective.[1] Here 'governance' means 'any attempt to control or manage any known object' (Hunt and Wickham, 1994: 78). This perspective takes seriously the notion that discursive governing logics or 'mentalities' (Wood and Shearing, 2006) are translated into and animate programmes and agents that imagine policing and securing conduct in myriad ways. Providing physical security in city cores is traditionally the realm of the public police, but is also increasingly associated with quasi-public and private authorities and providers that coexist, exchange resources and sometimes conflict with one another (Burris et al, 2005; Lippert and O'Connor, 2006; Wood and Shearing, 2006).

Ambassador programmes are associated with BIDs or similar entrepreneurial organisations, some of which are becoming more involved in security provision (Hoyt, 2005: 190; Lippert, 2007). While a neoliberal logic befits the private, entrepreneurial character of BIDs (Wilson, 2004), reference to this broad governmental logic alone fails to lay bare practices of ambassadors, including their links with the public police. It is inadequate to suggest consistent with this logic that ambassadors merely carry out the state's wishes 'at a distance' (Johnston and Shearing, 2003). Within recent influential theories of 'networked governance' (Wood and Shearing, 2006), the public police are in principle not necessarily involved in each network. However, the public police are nonetheless often found to adopt a vital role in security. As Crawford (2006a) has argued, if the public police are neither steering nor rowing – to borrow the well-worn nautical metaphor – they may well be anchoring others' security provision. For these reasons, police and the logics that shape their relations with other security auspices and providers such as ambassadors warrant special empirical attention. Rather than broad logics like neoliberalism, we seek out less grand(iose) logics[2] – of which we assert 'clean and safe' is an exemplar – that may better render these relations and practices intelligible. This approach necessitates examination of documents consonant with orthodox governmentality analyses (for example Rose and Miller, 1992), but also personal interviews that can reveal real or potential conflict and unauthorised practices. Thus, in this chapter, we reveal:

- ambassador strategies and practices;
- how ambassadors relate to police;
- how a 'clean and safe' rationality shapes and constitutes these practices and relations;
- how ambassadors operate relative to an increasingly complex assemblage of public, quasi-public and private auspices and providers.

The character of ambassador programmes and practices is linked to the nature of relations with the public police. These relations entail exchanging knowledge derived from street surveillance for some degree of training, limited affiliation and tacit tolerance. We identify practices of ambassadors to include:

- acting as 'eyes and ears' of police;
- policing 'nuisance' behaviour using indirect and unauthorised strategies, by establishing a visible presence and discreetly invoking law;
- providing physical security.

Derived from the 'broken windows' thesis (Wilson and Kelling, 1982) explained earlier in this book, we contend that 'clean and safe' is the governing logic through which ambassadors seek to provide security and transform the physical reality and imaginings of city centres. Accordingly, 'clean and safe' shapes ambassadors' relations with police, patrols for crime and 'nuisance' conduct, mass media communications and even personal appearance.

Previous research on 'ambassadors'[3] is limited. Ambassador programmes are occasionally discussed on the periphery of inquiries into urban policing and security. For example, a study of security arrangements in a BID in Vancouver, Canada, asserts that an implicit duty of downtown ambassadors is to patrol for crime and disorder (Huey et al, 2005). In response to disorderly conduct (for example, panhandling/begging) ambassadors are to encourage offenders to cease or relocate their behaviour. Armed with knowledge of the law and the local BID's permission to protect members' property, ambassadors threaten 'loitering' youth and homeless people with legal consequences when they refuse to comply with demands (Huey et al, 2005: 160-1). Mitchell and Staeheli (2006) similarly describe ambassadors' harassment of homeless people during privatisation of a city centre plaza in San Diego.

This previous research describes ambassadors as a form of private security predicated on creating environs consistent with the profit-driven interests of BIDs. Yet, much remains unknown about logics that shape ambassador practices, strategies and relations with police, as well as their broader implications for understanding urban security provision. We next discuss ambassador programme emergence and then focus on four overlapping elements: policing ambassadors' distance; 'eyes and ears' surveillance; a 'clean and safe' logic; and 'nuisance' strategies. We conclude by discussing theoretical implications of this analysis in relation to frontiers.

Research procedures

We analysed programme-specific documents, including procedure manuals, evaluations and operational documents, from three ambassador programmes in one Canadian province. We supplemented this with information collected about programmes in other cities, mostly in North America and the UK.[4] We examined city government websites, ambassador newsletters, BID annual reports, and print media accounts of BIDs and ambassador programmes.

To complement these procedures, 23 open-focused interviews were conducted. Interviewees were identified through BID offices, print media coverage and snowball techniques.[5] These included 10 ambassadors: seven women and three men, the majority in their 20s; and six supervisors, four from the three closely studied programmes and two from programmes in two major North American cities. The supervisors were responsible for hiring, managing and training ambassadors, and possessed institutional knowledge about practices and relations with police. Three police representatives, each linked to a specific ambassador programme by providing orientation or serving as a liaison, representatives of two BIDs without ambassador programmes, a city official who oversees BID relations, and a BID umbrella organisation in the three cities were also interviewed.

The three ambassador programmes closely studied here operate in small and mid-sized cities that are dependent on automobile and steel manufacturing and commodity production – economic sectors in steep decline. Their downtowns exhibit boarded-up and empty storefronts and have had trouble in retaining small businesses. A key way in which BIDs attempt to respond to such conditions and to foster increased consumption is through image improvement via 'streetscaping' enhancements, marketing events and intensive security provision (Hoyt, 2003).

Ambassador programmes are consonant with these mostly cosmetic developments, with one BID representative remarking in an interview that ambassadors would help to endow the city centre with a "new face" (BID Representative 2). In response to assumed aesthetic preferences of customers for private shopping malls, a BID-specific 'clean and safe' logic has formed in opposition to prevailing images of downtowns as comparatively dirty and dangerous.

This logic is promoted by the US-based International Downtown Association and is evinced in shifting revitalisation priorities. For example, its 'Downtown of the Month' promotion (which in March 2018 was Atlanta, Georgia) features the following on its webpage:

> The Downtown Ambassador Force and Clean Team ensure that Downtown is safe, clean and hospitable, and is on hand seven days a week throughout the central business district to provide directions, recommendations, escort service and maintenance. (International Downtown Association, 2018)

As one BID representative related:

> 'We're trying to figure out the clean and safe program ... we had an audit done of our organisation by the International Downtown Association and they said that most communities ... typically spend a third of their budget on clean and safe initiatives. So that would be things like the security cameras [and] the downtown ambassador program.' (BID Representative 2)

In one programme, ambassadors were operationally defined as a 'clean and safe' budgetary initiative by the BID, which formulaically devotes one third of its annual budget (consistent with International Downtown Association guidelines) towards 'clean and safe' (BID Representative 3). Since ambassador programmes tend to assume the majority of 'clean and safe' budget spending, BIDs' ambassador operations are potentially accorded considerable resources. Ambassadors are to guide visiting consumers and to provide services to local businesses, while actively patrolling for crime and 'nuisance' behaviour.

Of the three ambassador programmes studied closely, two operate with paid employment at, or slightly above, minimum wage (which is common for most ambassador programmes, Witsil, 2015), and one with volunteers. The programmes employ an average of eight ambassadors at a time. All three recruit postsecondary policing and criminology students, who complete from one to two weeks' training arranged by programme supervisors that typically includes customer service, tours of downtown visitor attractions, and communication protocol. Ambassadors also receive orientation from social service organisations and from the police. Before initiating these operations, BID representatives approached local police services to request operational support and approval.

Police–ambassador relations

Police seek to ensure that ambassadors avoid representing the police themselves or appearing as police or contract private security. The distinction between police and private security personnel, on the one hand, and ambassadors, on the other hand, is itself policed. To limit misperceptions, prior to police approving one ambassador programme, a police representative demanded restrictions on the uniform: "We ... wouldn't have supported the program if they were going to use any type of a security-type mandate, whether it be in their clothing or in a patch or any descriptor on their person" (Police Administrator 1). The primary prohibition is wearing shirt styles that smack of authority, like those worn by police and private security personnel. One ambassador programme went as far as to instruct ambassadors 'never [to] leave anyone with the impression that they are [police] or they may be subject to criminal charges for impersonating a police officer' (Manual 2). Yet, as discussed later, ambassadors exercise authority through their uniform's ambiguity and by feigning direct communication links to police.

Ambassador programme supervisors also deny that the programme is about security, yet suggest that ambassadors enhance 'safety' (not unlike community safety officers, discussed in Chapter Three). This distinction, which stems from a 'clean and safe' logic, is evinced in interviews with ambassador supervisors.

Interviewer: 'You wouldn't necessarily want private security guards in uniform walking around?'

Supervisor: 'Right. It's not private security. We're a safety presence, not security.'

Interviewer: 'It doesn't fall under ... private security regulations?'

Supervisor: 'No, no.' (Ambassador Supervisor 1)

Another supervisor was asked: Do these people also serve as security people?

Supervisor: 'Nope. That was one distinction that the police was very careful to make; that the ambassadors are not security. They are there to report if they see something happening but they are not to step in or mediate or anything like that ...'

Interviewer: 'So if they do see something they report it?'

Supervisor: 'Yes. They definitely report it ... But they are not to intervene or put themselves in harm's way'.

Interviewer: 'Is that consistent with other BIDs? It's not just the police here?'

Supervisor: 'No. When they are dealing with homeless people, I even tell them not to really engage them, because there's a liability issue for us if anything ever happened to ... the ambassador.' (Ambassador Supervisor 2)

A police liaison officer similarly remarked that this distance was vital for "liability-risk issues for the City, for the BID, and for the ambassadors themselves. It was important that they understood that security was not a component of their duties" (Police Administrator 2). Distance is established, then, due to direct police demands, but also ancillary benefits of avoiding – at least in the jurisdictions studied – governance through private security regulation and broader private insurance requirements impinging on BIDs to avoid liability exposure.

Despite this distance, the link between ambassadors and the police is nonetheless strategically implied by recruiters. Ambassadors are presumed to refine skills by serving in a security-related capacity. In one programme's manual, for example, the 'Benefits of Being an Ambassador' section lists the ability 'to hone new observational skills' (Manual 1). Despite denying that ambassadors are a form of security, one supervisor stated:

> 'The role of the ambassadors is to be always aware of everything that is going around them, like a police officer. It is the best training for a budding police officer to get because he's going to be walking a beat; he's going to make himself familiar with the areas that he's walking in …' (Ambassador Supervisor 3)

This same supervisor later remarked that among 'success stories' are at least two former ambassadors who became police officers and had gained pertinent experience through the programme (Ambassador Supervisor 3). Another supervisor from a volunteer-based operation tacitly admitted that the ambassador role befits a policing career (Ambassador Supervisor 1). This programme could only advertise community volunteering experience as participation incentive, yet provided notepads to young recruits cleverly referred to as 'evidence notebooks', thus evoking police imagery (Ambassador Supervisor 1).

Although no programme endorses ambassadors acting as police, as in the 'wannabe' culture of private security firms (Rigakos, 2002), potential recruits with police aspirations are at times promised opportunity to gain policing skills. In Winnipeg, the ambassador recruitment advertisement reads: 'Are you interested in law enforcement or criminal justice? This is a great opportunity to build skills and experience that can take you to the next level' (Winnipeg BIZ, 2018). For ambassador programmes to function, some – but not too much – distance needs to be maintained between police and ambassadors. To help recruit ambassadors, residue of the police – their authority and mystic – must to be left to linger. If the programme was cleansed of a police presence it would be far less attractive to would-be recruits who are looking for careers in policing or who wish to emulate police.

'Eyes and ears' surveillance

Policing and security provision are characterised by information gathering and sharing. Securing urban territories and populations correspondingly relies on increasing trade of knowledge (Ericson and Haggerty, 1997; Dupont, 2004). A rationale for public police departments to forge cooperative relationships with ambassadors, then, is to gather information about spatial and temporal patterns of activity on city streets.

As with police-dominated prevention programmes such as Crime Stoppers (for example, Lippert and Walby, 2017) that encourage relay of risk knowledge to police, ambassadors are often constituted through the bodily metaphor of 'eyes and ears'. Milwaukee, Wisconsin's programme website, for example, states that ambassadors 'serve as an extra set of eyes and ears for Milwaukee's police … [and] always have a pulse on what is happening' (Milwaukee Downtown, 2018). Information produced through visual and audio surveillance is to be transferred to, presumably, a police body and brain. Ambassadors are to transfer knowledge about identified problems quickly and consequently increase police response efficiency. In exchange, ambassador programmes are provided with police support, though to varying degrees. Police grant approval for ambassador programmes, which precedes the establishment of ambassador operations.

Ambassadors conduct surveillance for police and are listed in police documents and websites either as official 'partners' or affiliates. In addition to such general agreements, specific police rationales for relying on ambassadors as 'eyes and ears' surveillance include ambassadors' citizenship obligations. As citizens, ambassadors are assumed to be responsible to report unlawful occurrences to police, which from a police perspective justifies not granting ambassadors legal arrest or search powers. One police representative remarked that since downtown residents are especially apathetic about reporting crime, establishment of ambassador programmes was a hopeful turning point (Police Representative 1). Another said:

> 'Our community motto [is] "community partners", so we were very interested in any partnership that we could form … there was a rash of problems in the downtown core and one of the things we needed was extra "eyes and ears" … Now that we've become more mechanised there are less people out there, which means less "eyes and ears"'. (Police Representative 2)

Thus, police acknowledged the need for citizen assistance in reporting crime to respond to downtown problems.

This longstanding community policing emphasis (Johnston, 2003) imagines 'partners' taking responsibility and serving as a source of information for police. Yet, the practical scope of the ambassador–police relationship is limited. This is true of police training of ambassadors, which is either only one day or a few evening seminars. One police trainer indicated that training is provided voluntarily as a "one-off deal" (Police Representative 1). Moreover, besides addressing and providing ambassadors with information before major downtown events, police–ambassador relations tend to be devoid of regular consultation. Nor are ambassador patrols equipped with a special means of contacting police, such as a telephone contact number. Instead, ambassadors are to use emergency telephone numbers designed for the public.

Ambassadors reported two outlooks towards police. Some ambassadors expressed a distant acquaintance with beat officers, whereby they would greet officers on the street. However, several others complained that when crimes were reported, officers failed to take sufficient action. Ambassadors lamented that downtown police patrols lacked visibility, one claiming that officers regularly lounged at the back of downtown restaurants and cafes while supposedly 'on patrol' (Ambassador 4). Another ambassador recalled being mocked by veteran police officers as the "idiot in the coloured jacket" (Ambassador 3). Disrespect regarding their role was apparent to other ambassadors as well, who reported that police either disregarded them or deemed them to be "stepping on their toes" (Ambassador 6). These examples suggest that relations are not devoid of potential conflict. Typically, ambassador supervisors establish a stronger connection with police than their ambassador patrols.

Yet, aside from occasional consultation on an on-call basis, personal dealings with police supervisors are few. Police have no official oversight of ambassador operations (as might be expected if police were formally 'steering' ambassadors) and possess no special responsibility to supervisors. Though some personal exchanges occur, it is supervisors who regularly transfer knowledge derived from ambassador street surveillance to police. Either ambassadors or traditional private security are hired by BIDs or equivalent organisations to patrol downtown streets, not both. Few of the mostly small businesses in the cities studied independently hired private security to secure their premises (beyond alarm monitoring). Few information exchanges occur between ambassadors and private security. However, in a major North American city centre, in which both ambassadors operated and some larger businesses employed private security, crime alerts about "somebody getting out of jail, breaking into cars, [or] getting into garages" were regularly circulated. In that city core, police, ambassadors and private security were 'networked' via email, and monthly information-sharing meetings were held (Police Representative 4). Such expectations are also spelled out in manuals. When asked to explain 'eyes and ears', an ambassador supervisor related:

> 'You're walking down the street and there's the two of you … you're constantly assessing what's going on, in front of you, and behind you, and beside you. Okay, so your "eyes and ears" are all over the place. So if you see something coming at you down the street, and you feel in your gut that something's wrong, call it in or be on the look-out. Be aware. That's the "eyes and ears" of the police.' (Ambassador Supervisor 1)

Minor 'infractions', such as panhandling/begging, vandalism and graffiti, are to be relayed to ambassador supervisors. For panhandling, ambassadors tend to avoid calling police and instead merely note a description and location of the 'panhandler' and fill out a 'Suspect Identification Chart' on returning to base (Manual 3), thus collecting this information primarily for BID purposes.

To support this function, police typically provide training to ambassadors. One police department provides a plainclothes beat officer to prepare or 'street proof' ambassadors through a downtown familiarisation tour. Such a walk-about is intended to point out "where all the hot spots are, places to be aware of, places to avoid [and] places to have your antenna up when you're around" (Police Representative 1). Spaces where criminal and 'nuisance' conduct occur are to be figuratively illuminated for young ambassador eyes. This police trainer remarked that most ambassadors are naive about the rough and tumble nature of a downtown area that is "rife with transients, drugs, alcoholics, emotionally disturbed persons and … 'sex theatres' that becomes 'a freak show' after nine-to-five office workers leave for the suburbs" (Police Representative 1). Pointing out known areas of prostitution and illicit drug-dealing and consumption is thought to accustom ambassadors to unsettling conditions of city cores to be encountered later on patrol.

Policing the production of knowledge about conduct in specific spaces is equally vital. In one programme, ambassadors are taught surveillance-pertinent topics, including Canadian Criminal Code offence classification (Manual 2). Ambassadors are taught an informal protocol concerning the transfer of knowledge derived from observations at or near crime scenes in preferred police communication formats. In conjunction with knowledge of 'hotspots' and offences, ambassador training includes reporting protocol and the 911 emergency system. It is imagined that working knowledge of this system facilitates the mimicking of police communication procedures and streamlined, 'cleaner' reporting, with few questions required of the police dispatcher.

Ambassadors are also taught to be 'discreet observers' during patrols, to avoid singling out anyone and to walk at least half a block before calling police if witnessing a criminal incident (Police Representative 1). Such training is not only to aid ambassadors in avoiding detection and enhancing their personal safety, but also to ensure a reliable, controlled flow of information into police channels.

The transfer of information resulting from surveillance takes the form of statistical and intelligence reports. These reports lend credence to ambassadors' claims of serving as police 'eyes and ears'. Yet, not all crime-related information produced by ambassadors is actionable by police. The value of ambassadors' surveillance to police is evinced to derive from its contribution to immediate action and discernable results, for example spotting a person routinely loitering at a specific place and time, making hand-to-hand contact with an apparent stranger and then ducking into an alley (Police Representative 1). Yet long-term statistical summaries painstakingly compiled by supervisors using ambassadors' observational data from activity reports were sometimes ignored by police. For example, two of the key police representatives interviewed claimed never to have seen such reports. A third police representative claimed to use the reports to determine "areas of the city that we're having more problems with" (Police Representative 2). However, casting doubt on this claim that ambassador intelligence helped to identify crime 'hotspots' is that ambassadors in this city had inconsistent operational hours and often ended patrols at 9 pm, much earlier than the legally mandated bar closing time, when inebriated patrons exit onto downtown streets. Ambassador surveillance is deemed to be useful more when it leads to immediate arrests and less when the resulting statistical knowledge would ostensibly require significant modification of police patrol and prevention practices consistent with community policing initiatives.

'Clean and safe' frontiers

Problems encountered by ambassadors are rarely exclusively deemed to be 'clean' or 'safe'; instead, they routinely involve both of these goals. One supervisor described 'clean and safe' as the foundational building blocks of a refashioned, more appealing downtown:

'One of the most important things ... [is] a clean and safe environment for people to come to. It is absolutely necessary because if you don't feel clean and safe you're not going to have a good time, in anywhere you go, in any event.' (Ambassador Supervisor 1)

Garbage strewn about the curb or overflowing from receptacles is to be removed. Human faeces, vomit, used condoms, diapers, tampons, broken glass and syringes are assumed to create risk of disease or infection. These risky substances and barriers are among the materials that ambassadors report physically removing. However, the downtown is to become not so much 'risk-free', as more aesthetically pleasing. Garbage on the curb and graffiti on retail storefronts are presumed to generate an uninviting image, repelling those preferring the sanitised spaces of suburban malls and newer retail 'power centres', and to beget – in 'broken windows' thinking – further disorder.

Ambassadors also seek to locate and remove illegal and 'unsightly' postings such as advertisements, stickers and promotional flyers (Ambassador 5) – elements deemed to be linked to images of disorder. Ambassador patrols (informed and mobilised by a 'clean and safe' rationality) also include inspecting the front and back of downtown businesses for unsecured doors. When these are discovered, ambassadors contact BID headquarters to alert building owners and summon the police. Thus, ambassadors also engage directly in loss prevention practices on behalf of BID members, of a kind usually associated with private security or 'paid duty' public policing arrangements. One ambassador programme made its patrolling pairs available to anyone requesting escort to a vehicle in a downtown parking garage (Manual 1).

Thus, 'clean' anticipates not only the physical but also the social cleansing of downtown (Kennelly, 2015) – the removal of manifestations of social problems deemed to be nuisance behaviour and which BIDs presume reflect negatively on a city centre's character.

A focus on panhandling/begging

Panhandling/begging is a preoccupation of ambassadors as it is deemed to impede consumption activity and pedestrian flow both symbolically and physically. A supervisor remarked: "That is one of the biggest problems ... what gives the perception of being unsafe and not clean – the panhandlers" (Ambassador Supervisor 1).

BIDs have developed an array of means to manage panhandlers and assorted expertise that local government and public police would not openly acknowledge or publicly discuss. Although restricted from self-representing as police or licensed private security guards, at times ambassadors nonetheless use such appearances to their advantage. Ambassadors approach panhandlers to thwart their begging requests to passing pedestrians. In one major BID in the US, the programme coordinator related:

> 'They're taught homeless intervention, panhandling intervention. [If] someone's panhandling at the corner, we can go and stand next to them and we can ask them to move along. A police officer cannot do that, it's a violation … Street panhandling is freedom of speech [if you] simply stand on the corner and ask for money or stand in front of a businessman's door asking for money, is not a violation of law. And the police cannot do anything about that … But we have the same freedom of speech because we have no authority. No arrest powers, no summoning power, we have no power. We are citizens.' (Ambassador Coordinator 1)

Ambassador presence and subtle cajoling is not about immediate coercion. Rather, it is an indirect, subtler reminder of possible police coercion, should ambassadors become targets of retaliation from those they watch and annoy on city centre sidewalks and in public spaces.

In Winnipeg, ambassadors have focused to a great extent on Indigenous people, who panhandle in the downtown. The panhandlers there refer to the ambassadors – in an ironic allusion to the earlier North West Mounted Police's red serge uniforms as they engaged in the 'march west' to help 'settle' the frontier (see Chapter Seven) – as the 'Red Coats' (Public Interest Law Centre, 2007). Panhandlers reported that 'the ambassadors tell them to "move along", or "[w]e don't want to see your face down here"'. After a new anti-panhandling bylaw had been passed in Winnipeg, interviews with panhandlers revealed that: 'Most respondents who felt there had been a change … said the BIZ ambassadors had become more "harassing now" and tell them to move along regardless of where they are panhandling, or actually tell them to quit panhandling altogether' (Public Interest Law Centre, 2007: 51-2).

In another city, the BID formed a panhandling 'task force', with the aim of eradicating panhandling. One BID paid representatives from the first Canadian ambassador programme to visit its downtown to informally evaluate the feasibility of implementing a similar programme. Their resulting review was glowing, except for highlighting the prevalence of panhandling. The BID then prioritised panhandling and assigned to ambassadors the task of reducing it (Ambassador Supervisor 1). Ambassadors in one programme became so adept at generating statistical knowledge in the city centre, that the BID directed ambassadors to commence gathering information to persuade the local city council to enact a new panhandling bylaw.

The media image

Managing image is central to being 'clean and safe'. Ambassador supervisors do not advertise incidents of verbal and physical assaults on ambassadors (reported in anonymous interviews). Consistent with this, a 'clean and safe' logic also informs interactions between ambassadors and the media.

A common feature of programmes is recognition that ambassadors need public relations instruction. One manual devotes two and a half pages to handling media interviews, including how to avoid misinterpretation and misquoting. Ambassadors are advised to keep responses 'five to fifteen seconds long' and to 'resist the urge to elaborate' if the interviewer is silent following a response to avoid distortion (Manual 1). Thus, there is a sense in which ambassador interactions with the media are also to be 'clean and safe'.

Another aspect of media relations training deals with how best to 'spin' responses, to conjure up imaginings of a safe city core:

> In your answers, your first-person testimonial about what you see and do should support the fact that Downtown is a safe place to visit. You don't necessarily need to say the word "safe," let the reporter make that conclusion based on your comments. It will come through much stronger in the story if it's an observed fact, rather than a direct quote from you. (Manual 1)

Interviews are opportunities to 'help' the media conclude that the city centre is safe for consumption. Ambassadors seek physical security, but also to represent city centres as safe to wider publics.

Ambassadors as targets

Ambassadors are not only agents of a 'clean and safe' policy, but also its targets. Ambassadors are to be the human embodiment of a 'clean and safe' logic that fashions ambassadors' young bodies and habits. There is a sense in which ambassadors are designed into the downtown environments with 'clean and safe' becoming a goal of ambassadors' bodies and habits too. Ambassadors are to be this logic's human incarnation. Thus, ambassador programmes typically require ambassadors to concern themselves with a 'clean' personal appearance and prohibit them from wearing any attire other than bright, officially sanctioned uniforms.

These requirements seek to contrast ambassadors (many of whom are in their 20s, based on interviews and programme documents, including website images) with the youth whose conduct they are to watch. Through police and other training, ambassadors are encouraged to remain personally 'safe' in everyday work practices. For example, they are not to actively provoke panhandlers or to patrol alone.

Programme requirements prohibit adorning ambassadors with jewellery (dangling chains, earrings, bracelets) or penetrating skin with lip or eyebrow hoops or studs. Even specific nail and hair conditions of ambassadors' bodies are forbidden (false nails, nail polish, dirty nails, hair extensions, untied hair past the shoulders and facial hair; Manual 3). Ambassadors' uniformed bodies are to embody the 'clean and safe' image of this new urban landscape, to at once cleanse and blend with an idealised physical and social refuse-free retail realm.

Strategies for eradicating nuisance behaviours

Ambassadors seek to encourage consumption in the BID and to deter behaviour that might create a sense of insecurity or otherwise damage the ongoing remaking of the downtown's image. Ambassadors use specific strategies to eradicate 'nuisance' behaviours.

Providing a uniformed presence

Consistent with a 'clean and safe' rationality that targets ambassadors' bodies are ambassadors' uniforms. Wearing matching, brightly coloured clothing and patrolling as pedestrian pairs, ambassadors are highly visible, their uniforms creating an image of an unnamed civil authority thought capable of deterring undesirable behaviour. Ambassadors rely on their uniform's ambiguity to advantage:

> 'At one of the downtown stores we would go in and do a walk-through because they have a lot of theft issues, but they don't employ security ... The management loved it because it was a deterrent to anybody who might think "Oh shit, there's some guy in a uniform". Once they see

that you're in uniform they just process the fact that you're
a cop automatically.' (Ambassador 3)

Despite the policing of ambassadors' boundaries discussed earlier, if
a potential violator might be "less likely to do something in front of
us", ambassadors approved of being mistaken for private security or
'a cop'. The foremost way in which ambassadors seek to counteract
nuisance is via their visible street *presence* (this is an emphasis of 'users'
who pay for extra public police too – see Chapter Seven), but without
connoting that downtown spaces are unsafe and to be avoided. For
one downtown experiencing 'loitering', a supervisor remarked that
ambassadors demonstrate "a presence in the downtown, that we are
not going to have people intimidating our customers and people who
are using our services" (Ambassador Supervisor 3).

For a police representative, ambassadors deter 'loiterers', by
"stand[ing] around them and ... making them uncomfortable by your
presence", suggesting they would "move them along, just by their
presence" (Police Representative 2). Ambassadors in one programme
use the following tactic: they move close to panhandlers and talk to
persons to whom the panhandler is requesting a gift of money, in a
bid to thwart the panhandler's requests. Ambassadors and a supervisor
described this as 'educating' the panhandler's 'target', with messages
like "[p]lease don't; he's a regular". Ambassadors explain to consumers
that the downtown has soup kitchens and social services, and warn of
exacerbating panhandlers' problems.

Ambassadors' capacity for deterrence through presence is nonetheless
deemed to have limits. When encountering drug deals on the street,
for example, ambassadors indicate that their presence merely displaced
or delayed transactions. Police equate ambassador presence to crime
prevention through environmental design tactics that seek to prevent
crime through location-specific methods. In discouraging 'loitering'
without being "overt and moving them off", ambassadors' presence is
imagined to be vital to securing the city centre (Police Representative
2). The BID-funded ambassador presence is neither immediate
coercion nor a sign of dangerous space. Rather, it is a subtle reminder
of police coercion that waits on the horizon as a 'background asset'
(Crawford, 2006b: 136).

Invoking the law

Unlike in the 'mass private properties' (Shearing and Stenning, 1981)
of suburban malls, BIDs' efforts to eliminate human disorder occur

in public space. Since access to public space for panhandling cannot be legally restricted in Canadian jurisdictions (Hermer and Mosher, 2002), and due to pressure from the BID and police to avoid explicitly doing so (consistent with the 'clean and safe' rationale), another key ambassador strategy is to invoke the law in how they provide security – obliquely and unofficially.

Ambassadors request that violators cease or move their behaviour elsewhere, while invoking knowledge of legal regulations. The laws invoked tend to centre on nuisance issues deemed to be barriers to ramping up consumption at BID businesses. Among these are city bylaws related to: illegal postings such as advertisements, stickers and promotional flyers; skateboarding, bicycling and rollerblading on sidewalks; loitering; smoking near building entrances; spitting; and littering.

One police representative related teaching Ontario's Trespass to Property Act (2009) and the Ontario Safe Streets Act (1999) to ambassadors (Police Representative 2), but ambassadors dispute this in interviews. Despite not knowing the latter provincial statute, ambassadors recognise 'aggressive' panhandling to be illegal. Although ambassadors could discern a legal violation, they often lack knowledge of the name or content of the relevant law. When asked if they enforce law, ambassadors and supervisors indicate that such action is not within their powers. Yet, in interviews when specific nuisances are discussed, invocation of the law is invariably mentioned as a strategy to deal with these problems.

To stop prohibited activities, ambassadors deploy a variation of the word 'law' in the first few words of an utterance when speaking to identified violators. By saying '[b]y law you're not allowed ...' or '[t]here's a bylaw ...', ambassadors report achieving compliance in some situations. When asked if she considered this to be law enforcement, one ambassador replied that she is "just notifying them" that "you could get fined if you do that" (Ambassador 10).

Ambassadors also report coupling this approach with speaking apologetically: "We're really sorry but you know you're not allowed to do this. Just legally you can't do this" (Ambassador 6). Ambassadors are cognisant of avoiding coarse or authoritarian orders associated with the police – commands like 'move it', 'move on' or 'get off the sidewalk' – which are thought to risk a hostile response. Such practices are not discussed in manuals or training. Invoking the law is unofficial and informal.

Despite safety concerns, and a lack of official endorsement, ambassadors commonly report moderate results from invoking the law.

For panhandling, ambassadors often find this tactic to be ineffective – panhandlers tended to be unfazed by legal threats coupled with polite requests to cease their conduct. Yet for illegal postings, ambassadors found success in invoking the law. Ambassadors reported stopping violators taping advertisements, stickers and promotional flyers to BID property. When told that their posting was illegal, some perpetrators heeded the warning. One ambassador described tracking the same perpetrator down the street and removing each posting one by one (Ambassador 9). Invocation of the law occasionally shifted upward to supervisors. When an excessive number of posters from one business was discovered, one supervisor called the business to invoke the bylaw (Ambassador Supervisor 1).

Aside from these two points of intervention, ambassador law-invoking usually targets youths performing skateboarding and bike tricks on sidewalks, which is deemed to be damaging to public infrastructure and private property – and a barrier to pedestrian flow and consumption. Since most violators are youths, ambassadors seek compliance by trying to "talk to them on their level" (Ambassador 3). An ambassador recalled an incident when he first politely reminded a violator that the sidewalk was not a skateboard park and suggested skateboarding at a park located elsewhere. This ambassador remarked how an authoritative command like "get off" would result: "now he's going to go down along the sidewalk five feet then jump back onto the sidewalk just to piss you off, or just to say 'What are you going to do to me?'" (Ambassador 3).

A related strategy of dealing with this 'nuisance' involves the ambassador communication system. One supervisor remarked: "[N] uisance-wise ... their best weapon, their best tool to exert authority was their radio" (Ambassador Supervisor 1). Where ambassadors encountered young skateboarders forced from a publicly sanctioned downtown skateboarding spot by older youth, the supervisor described telling the ambassadors:

> 'Call it in. They don't know who you're calling it in to. So you sound official and say ... Ambassador to Base. What is Base? Especially to kids that are harassing, the skateboarders or ... panhandlers or whatever it's Ambassador-to-Base, Ambassador-to-Base ... "You'd better leave or you will be reported. I am reporting you right now. Ambassador-to-Base" ... It worked like magic. There was never a situation that escalated to where we needed to call the police and that

is why I can say it was a [valuable] method of deterring.'
(Ambassador Supervisor 1)

One ambassador reported feigning turning on his radio and keying into headquarters: "[T]he minute you said on the radio maybe 'Call the police', they were afraid … whenever they heard that they used to take off. And that was that" (Ambassador 4). Feigning contact with an authority at 'home base' or to police, while not directly invoking law, nonetheless are strategies befitting 'clean and safe' institutional arrangements discussed earlier.

Consistent with policing of boundaries between police and ambassadors, the police claim to be entirely against ambassadors invoking the law to confront nuisances.

Police representative: 'Ambassadors are not to engage anybody that they may have perceived to have been committing any type of criminal act … not even to approach a situation that, in their opinion, could be a criminal act'.

Interviewer: 'Would that also include any less serious crimes like nuisance issues such as panhandling?'

Police representative: 'Yes … those issues may seem insignificant … but for persons who do not have the authority to engage a panhandler or to engage somebody else who's committing inappropriate behaviour does not mean that that cannot escalate into a more serious situation … They're not trained for it; it's not their mandate … If they see something like that, call the police, let us engage those people.' (Police Representative 3)

Another police representative said that ambassadors are oblivious to physical and health dangers of attempting to encourage persons to 'move on', especially due to possible hidden weapons and communicable diseases (Police Representative 1). All police representatives emphasised that ambassadors lack the legal authority to engage persons and the capability to deal properly with nuisances. One noted:

'Once someone calls bullshit on you, you can't back down. So if you tell somebody to move along, and they say "We're not moving, you don't have the authority to move us", and you don't, now what do you do? And now you've really lost any of your [authority]… right?' (Police Representative 2)

For the police, ambassadors' law enforcement assistance is inappropriate; summoning law oversteps the ambassador's role, treads on police territory, and risks becoming a nuisance to the police, should a hostile reaction occur to which they must respond.

Conclusions

Like more regulated private security, ambassadors develop ways to achieve goals by using 'less overtly coercive tools' (Mopas and Stenning, 2001: 69). Despite providing security, it is ambassadors' ambiguous appearance that ironically sets them apart. The security provided is neither self-evident nor easily distinguishable from other ambassador practices. Hiring young, 'clean-cut' persons and insisting that they seamlessly and safely merge with the beautification of downtown spaces they patrol is intended to create a welcoming atmosphere for preferred consumers. This aesthetic enhancement entails restrictions on personal appearance, such that ambassadors become mobile human signs of a 'clean and safe' city centre, an image similarly channelled through mass media, and all at a cost far less than deployment of equal numbers of public police (but see also Chapter Seven).

Ambassador patrols are different from other policing and security agents in the pace and tempo of their work. This is consistent with proceeding obliquely and unofficially; they have a 'beat' like public police in some cities, but they proceed slowly on foot (not in cars or on horseback and rarely on bicycles). They are prepared to stop to give directions or consumer advice about city centre events or shops, to make observations, or to talk to skateboarders or young people in the manner described earlier. There are no rapid reactions to calls or complaints, and their value is not measured by speed. We return to this issue of temporality in the book's conclusion.

Within an emerging security market that is increasingly reliant on deterrence via visible presence in public space (Brown and Lippert, 2007), uniformed ambassadors are deemed to be valuable, because they can be tailored to the idiosyncratic contours of local downtowns. Ambassadors are a new gradation of policing and security provision, but one that strategically denies the designation and allegiance to the state or the private security industry. Ambassadors' hybrid security and marketing role promises to avoid negative public images of their private security guard counterparts (for example poorly trained, aggressive and unaccountable). To understand these practices, it is necessary to push the boundaries of criminology and to draw from urban studies and the sociology of governance.

A noteworthy exception to the typical lack of opposition to BID ambassadors, but one which proves the rule, concerns one of the few Canadian ambassador programmes in Vancouver, staffed by a private security firm that equips patrols with direct access to the police (Huey et al, 2005), thus rendering patrols more identifiable as traditional private security. This Vancouver BID's ambassador programme was subject to a human rights complaint from a legal society that advocates for homeless people. It alleged that ambassadors engage in discrimination when 'harassing' homeless people – a population disproportionately comprising Indigenous people as well as physically and mentally disabled people – by ordering them to stay off sidewalks and away from designated public areas. This ended with a ruling against the ambassadors for damages (CBC, 2015). This example is one among many that reveals our third meaning of frontiers concerning the targeting of Indigenous people at work in the operations of BID ambassadors.

Ambassador programmes are increasingly appearing in city centres and are fashioned and made possible through a 'clean and safe' logic. To get to this frontier, we have used research techniques that reveal the varied practices of BID ambassadors in all their complexity. Ambassador security provision, consistent with a 'clean and safe' logic, is made possible by this sometimes strategically exposed tether between ambassador and police. Ambassador programme avoidance of an explicit security designation – this 'clean and safe' security – may be broadly consistent with 'neoliberalism' or 'advanced liberalism' (Brady and Lippert, 2016) that imagines less regulated (that is, unlicensed) and correspondingly more market-driven forms of (cheaper) security labour. Yet, elaboration of 'clean and safe' logic on its own makes ambassador practices and relations with public police more intelligible. Other unearthed logics undoubtedly shape and make possible other vital linkages and practices within policing and security contexts, and therefore deserve empirical attention on urban frontiers the world over.

Notes

[1] This perspective overlaps with 'governmentality studies' (Brady and Lippert, 2016).

[2] In the sociology of governance, relying on neoliberalism as an explanation of practices is seen to overlook contingencies and nuances (Rose et al, 2006; Brady and Lippert, 2016).

[3]   Similar programmes use the terms 'host', 'customer service representative' or 'public safety guide' rather than 'ambassador'. We use 'ambassador' here for consistency. Greater detail about cities in which the three programmes operate was omitted, to ensure the anonymity of interviewees.

[4]   Operational documents included a presentation about one programme's operations, police training materials and daily activity report sheets. To avoid revealing the location of the ambassador programmes and the identity of interviewees, cited documents are referred to here as Manuals 1, 2 and 3.

[5]   Names of interviewees and cities were anonymised.

SIX

Public Corporate Security Officers and the Frontiers of Knowledge and Credentialism

Introduction

In this chapter, we examine public corporate security work. We focus on corporate security in 16 of Canada's municipal governments – referred to throughout the chapter as municipal corporate security (MCS) – and discuss how public corporate security has entered Canada's federal government departments. Conceiving of public corporate security as a new frontier of security provision, we show how it has become part of policing and security networks, as well as how knowledge, technology and strategies from the private security and insurance industries are being transferred into public government.

Engaging with sociologies of networked security governance, security consumption and risk management, we argue that public corporate security contributes to the securitisation of spaces through asset protection, risk and liability management, and employee surveillance. We discuss how the work of MCS specifically is animated by a discourse of urban threat, showing how MCS practices in Canadian cities blur the line between policing and securitisation. We also consider the implications of our analysis of public corporate security for understandings of policing, security and public accountability on the frontier of knowledge and credentialism. The latter refers to the increased and at times over-valuing of security educational credentials and the growing demand for them for corporate security work (see also Collins, 1979).

New urban security arrangements involving MCS are perhaps best symbolised by an unnamed official routinely watching a pre-screened employee sign for a plastic card allowing access to a newly restricted, non-public urban zone, with pre-screening and zoning determined using assessment tools from the private corporate world. MCS entails uploading a corporate-style arsenal of specialised knowledge, technology and strategy to regulate municipal workers, 'corporate assets' and properties. This inevitably also engages disadvantaged people living on the streets or near these properties.

MCS securitising aspirations are starting to transform city-owned and leased edifices as well as public spaces like parks, squares and streets used by urban dwellers. MCS departments are implicated in:

- surveillance for major public events (which entails threat assessments);
- securitisation of municipal buildings and property;
- dealing with 'broken windows' and other forms of 'nuisance', for example liquor consumption as well as homeless people (who in Western Canadian cities especially are disproportionately represented by Indigenous peoples) on municipal property;
- legal liability management.

Since 2001, at least 16 Canadian cities have introduced MCS departments. These units typically have a manager and three to five supervisors in charge of key practices, such as physical security, employee surveillance, and auditing and asset protection. These personnel are increasingly being expected to have new credentials designed for private sector corporate security, thus representing a new frontier in the arrival of these credentials and related knowledge, technology and strategy. In this chapter, we explore the rise of MCS departments with three overlapping purposes:

- First, we trace the emergence of MCS to determine the degree to which, and how, it has entered Canadian governments.
- Second, we explore the scope and nature of MCS practices as well as knowledge and technology transfer that activate MCS. We aim to trouble assumptions about the difference between policing and securitisation and thus about the capacity of a single sociological literature to account for these practices.
- Third, we seek to raise questions about the public accountability of MCS.

Insecurity is an issue that deeply concerns local, regional and federal authorities, engendering coordination among many public and private agencies (also see Jones and Newburn, 2006; Loader and Walker, 2007). In the US, municipal security provision has been shaped by the rise of Homeland Security and the pervasive 'War on Terror' (Marcuse, 2004; Caruson and MacManus, 2006; Walby and Lippert, 2015a). We argue that MCS has arrived in Canadian cities via three converging channels: the international private security industry, the international and domestic insurance industry; and other MCS managers/departments already present in Canadian cities. The vessels of this transfer include insurance industry workshops, an array of security commodities such as handbooks, the American Society for Industrial Security (ASIS International), and communication among MCS personnel.

In analysing MCS practices and knowledge and technology transfer, we contribute to debates about policing and securitisation (also see Wood and Dupont, 2006; Lippert and Walby, 2013), by questioning this distinction. If policing is the maintenance of order (Hermer et al, 2005) and securitisation means the regulation and fortification of buildings, spaces and things (Aradau, 2010), then MCS provides an example of regulatory work in which policing and securitisation merge but on a new frontier of public government rather than private corporations. In some cities, MCS investigates employee conduct and adopts a proactive risk management (securitisation typically understood as one method of risk management) approach towards securitising assets; whereas in other centres, MCS is (so far) involved only in the latter. MCS also coordinates with, and contracts out, private security for events. By targeting persons, conduct and things or assets, MCS troubles the dichotomy of reactive policing and proactive securitisation. In this sense too, with their novel credentials and practices, MCS personnel represent another frontier of security work.

First, we draw together sociological literatures on networked security, security consumption, and risk management to conceptualise MCS. After remarking on method, we chart the establishment of MCS in Canadian cities and analyse practices of its officers. Next, we emphasise knowledge and technology transfer and risk management, and explore the discourse of urban 'threat' in exemplifying and enabling MCS-related processes. Finally, in the discussion, we assess the implications of MCS for conceptualising policing and securitisation and the prospects of MCS accountability to the public. We also show how similar trends are developing at the federal level of government in Canada, including the department that is tasked with overseeing the lives of Indigenous peoples in Canada. MCS is, in principle, subject to the authority of city councillors and is dependent on other network agencies. However, through the importation of a security imaginary and a precautionary logic that amplifies the 'corporate-style' governance of cities (Rose, 2000), MCS becomes difficult for people outside the network to scrutinise, including the citizens of the cities in which MCS is expanding.

Making sense of municipal corporate security

The idea of 'corporate security' recalls investigative and auditing powers in private organisations. For instance, Gill and Hart (1999) discuss how private investigators within corporations monitor workers and manage intelligence leaks and theft. Power (2004) likewise discusses regulation within the private corporate world involving risk management and accounting (see also Johnston and Shearing, 2003: 75-97; Ericson, 2007: 122-54).

MCS is responsible for auditing municipal government units, tracking inventory and investigating asset loss. Although MCS work is like that of private security agencies, MCS is on the frontier of new developments, because it is a public, municipal government unit and, in principle, accountable to the citizenry. To make the development of MCS intelligible, we connect three related literatures:

- We draw from the governance of security literature (Crawford, 2006a; Wood and Dupont, 2006).
- This is combined with insights from sociological writings on security consumption and 'marketisation' (Brown and Lippert, 2007; Lippert and Walby, 2014; Walby and Lippert, 2015a).
- Finally, we draw from the sociological literature on risk and insurance as governance (Ericson and Doyle, 2004a; Baker, 2010).

Combining insights from these overlapping literatures is necessary to make sense of MCS; no single literature can fully explain the rise of public corporate security, which is a point we address in this and the concluding chapter. Here we discuss each literature in turn.

First, the governance of security literature focuses on networks of policing and security agencies (Johnston and Shearing, 2003; Shearing and Wood, 2003). The concepts of 'networks' and 'nodes' provide a starting point for conceptualising how policing and security agencies coordinate, cooperate and sometimes compete for status and resources (Johnston and Shearing, 2010). No single complex of nodes is granted primacy in analysis from this perspective. Public and private agencies cooperate in networks, and diverse styles of security governance are found throughout. What is important here is demonstrating logics by which nodes govern; technologies and techniques used to achieve goals; resources they access; as well as the always morphing organisational structure in which security governance is conducted (Dupont, 2004). Non-state agencies are not simply activated by the state. MCS provides an example of a security community that is partially 'activated' by the international private security and insurance industries and their approach towards legal liability and asset protection. Drawing from the nodal governance literature, we identify ties between MCS and the private security and insurance industries as a way of conceptualising MCS in policing and security networks.

Second, the sociological literature on security consumption focuses on governments as purchasers and consumers (rather than providers) of private security expertise and products. Security is now treated as a commodity that is bought and sold (Newburn, 2001; White, 2010), and sometimes contested (Loader and White, 2018), with a fluctuating market price. Goold et al (2010) assert that research on security consumption should focus on the supply side and demand sides, while Loader (1999) argues that new security communities are created by the push and pull of security supply and demand. MCS is one of these new security communities. Agencies that fail to protect their assets fail in security governance and are seen as flawed consumers by other nodes. There are expectations of MCS units to 'keep up' with trends in security consumption, and the major security conferences and expositions (for example, ASIS International meetings) allow for 'visits to the marketplace' (Crawford, 2006b: 111), where transfer of technology and knowledge as special corporate security credentials begins. Technology forms a large segment of the security industry (Brodeur, 2010), yet its transfer on policing and security frontiers, such as public corporate security, remains understudied.

Third, the sociological literature on risk and insurance examines governance and surveillance in the corporate sector. It explains the emergence of liability and precaution as prevalent logics of governing employees and steering the overall trajectory of organisations (Caruson and MacManus, 2006; Baker, 2010). This literature lends understanding to MCS insofar as MCS represents a corporate style of managing and monitoring municipal assets, workers and properties in public government. Management of risk requires knowledge of risk, which leads to auditing, measuring and assessments (Amoore and de Goede, 2005). The concern for liability and asset protection promotes the calculation of costs and damages. Risk management becomes a form of control that resets standards for employee conduct and municipal property use. This chapter contributes to this literature, by focusing on the neglected frontier of public, municipal government and its relations with insurance companies and its risk management strategies through MCS.

Research procedures

MCS departments rarely represent their practices on the webpages of municipal governments. They have low visibility compared to public police and private security. Consistent with Chapter Two, we therefore submitted a series of freedom of information (FOI)[1] requests to obtain information about MCS departments in 16 Canadian cities: Victoria and Vancouver (British Columbia), Edmonton and Calgary (Alberta), Saskatoon and Regina (Saskatchewan), Winnipeg (Manitoba), Ottawa, Oshawa, Brampton, Mississauga, Hamilton, Kitchener, Toronto (Ontario), Montréal (Quebec), and Halifax (Nova Scotia). We asked for official job descriptions, governing protocol and current project reports, to assemble an account of how MCS work is organised, the rationales through which it is animated, and the tasks involved. We asked for annual reports, budgets and itemised expenditure lists, to learn about the development and growth of MCS and how – and to whom – it accounts for its actions. Using FOI requests, we produced over 1,200 pages of documentation about MCS practices across Canada.

We supplemented this primary research strategy with several others. We analysed ASIS International, Canadian Security Association (CSA) and Canadian Society for Industrial Security (CSIS) products and private security marketing materials, including websites and trade journals (for example, *Canadian Security*, *Security Management*) to understand how products are marketed to MCS. We examined insurance exchange websites containing information about municipal liability insurance increases and risk management initiatives. In addition, we examined city council minutes from the mid-1990s to 2010 in cities for which this information was available, to locate decisions to approve creation of corporate security departments or major expenditures. To supplement and confirm the FOI material, we conducted 30 interviews with MCS personnel who oversee the operations in each city across Canada, as well as their various staff. Finally, to further explore risk and liability issues, we interviewed two municipal risk managers, a representative of a major non-profit municipal insurance exchange that provides insurance to municipalities, and representatives of two private risk mitigation companies.

In analysing these FOI materials and other data, we focused on the rationales for establishment and practices of MCS in Canadian cities. We analysed themes such as cooperation with other policing and security agencies, and the construction of 'threat' in MCS reports. Our FOI requests account for 16 (80%) of Canada's 20 largest municipalities by population. Three of the other five municipalities are covered with interviews and document analysis.

The arrival of municipal corporate security in Canada

Public corporate security, including MCS, has its origins in the private corporate world. In Canada and the US, cities are corporations, a fact that has doubtlessly made transfer of the 'corporate security' moniker seamless through slippage in the meaning of 'corporate'. The division between cities and businesses was established by the courts in the 19th century, when 'cities became sharply defined public, political entities', differentiated from private business corporations (Frug, 2001: 155). MCS raises questions about this longstanding distinction. MCS departments are housed in different types of municipal branches. Thus, it is difficult to locate where MCS will be situated in each municipal government structure, and not easy to pinpoint when the rise of MCS started.

We found little evidence of MCS departments and personnel in place before 2001, but there are several 2004 references to MCS departments in cities such as Vancouver, Edmonton and Toronto. The cities of Oshawa, Halifax, Brampton and Kitchener created MCS during or after 2006. Rising budget figures for MCS also signal the expansion of MCS across Canada. In this chapter, we explore this emerging pattern of knowledge and technology transfer from international private security industries to municipalities and increasing expenditures on technology and insurance in Canadian cities.

Security industry marketing to municipalities

While the growth of the private security industry and diversification of policing can, to some extent, be explained by increasing public demand for safety (White, 2010), this explanation works less well for the rise of MCS departments, which the public is not generally cognizant of. As the private security industry grows, and security becomes increasingly commodified, new markets (Haggerty, 2003; Loader and White, 2018) are being created on the policing and security frontier.

Security consumption

If municipalities were previously untapped markets, they are fast becoming targeted markets for the private security industry. MCS is affected by trends in security consumption, which is the first major influence on MCS incorporation and expansion in Canadian cities. Security consumption entails access to a privileged marketplace, such as ASIS International events and expositions. ASIS is an international organisation involved in security policy formation and circulation as well as accreditation.

Marketing strategies of these organisations see municipal governments as buyers and security providers. ASIS provides a 'total' security credential and strategy package for MCS activities, while CSA and CSIS are more 'hardware' or technology-oriented. Thus, the security industry market is differentiated, as MCS consumers attend events and engage various other agencies for different security needs.

MCS managers become experts on procurement and act as the relay point for knowledge transfer between private security and municipal government. They are vital brokers, who directly access the international scale for knowledge and technology to be used on a local level.

Credentialism and case studies

The qualifications for MCS managers and staff are also implicated in the accreditation criteria that organisations like ASIS promote. This reflects growing credentialism. To be eligible for positions with Halifax MCS, for example, an applicant needs a two-year college degree in security management plus five years of field experience and two years' investigation experience. The pedagogical materials are drawn either directly from (or are sponsored by) ASIS, CSA and CSIS. For Ottawa MCS, for example, an applicant needs ASIS accreditation. From ASIS, the Certified Protection Professional (CPP) designation has become key. As one MCS manager put it: "I think the CPP is a really valuable one to have. I've done it, my staff is currently going through to get certified." As another security manager put it: "With this particular organization, I couldn't get the job without a CPP".

Knowledge transfer is not just one-way: MCS field knowledge also regularly enters the security network through MCS managers. One MCS manager from Ontario provides training to other MCS personnel at ASIS conferences. Similarly, one MCS manager's account of the effects of introducing a new Proactive Audio Video (PAV) camera surveillance system in Ottawa's extensive series of parks and swimming pools is then appropriated by private security firms as a 'case study' to further market in trade journals and websites the component technologies that comprise this PAV system (for example, Dieser, 2007; Dedicated Micros, 2008). Thus, Pelco Spectra uses the MCS manager's story to market its 'dome cameras and loud speakers', and in a separate effort, the UK-based Dedicated Micros uses the same 'case study' to market its 'Digital Video Recorder' that banks the images. In each case, the legitimacy of Ottawa MCS in providing security for a nation's capital, and the MCS manager's account, are used by private agencies in the network to market their wares.

Policy transfer

The influence of international security industry knowledge on the field of MCS in Canada is evident in the citations to ASIS publications in MCS documents. For instance, all quotations under 'Research' for Halifax MCS are drawn from private security trade journals (that is, *Canadian Security*), ASIS-produced books, and US-based handbook material for corporate managers. The City of Toronto uses six 'ASIS' Publications (City of Toronto, 2009: 57, FOI: 83), including and especially the 'ASIS General Security Risk Assessment Guidelines' (City of Toronto, 2009: 16; FOI: 42). These examples of policy transfer are part of a trend of borrowing security technologies and emulating innovations from other municipalities. MCS measures are adopted by copying policies and handbooks (MCS Manager 1). With that transfer comes embedded assumptions and metaphors that are potentially at odds with local and even national (for example, Canadian) cultures and public accountability at the new destination.

These examples of transfer of specific knowledge and technology from the private security industry to Canadian municipal government signal the rise of MCS as a security market. The primary focus of research on public policy transfer has been how federal government agencies learn from one another (MIABC, 2004). Policy makers weigh the pros and cons of innovative policy initiatives, before endorsing a new policy position (Nicholson-Crotty, 2009). Mintrom (1997) introduces the notion of 'policy entrepreneurs' to understand how political actors place items on government agendas, suggestive of how individual actors play a key role in amplifying a policy's value.

MCS is different, in that the transfer is mostly from international private security agencies to local public governments and between municipalities. For MCS, managers attend international security expositions that are chief sites for knowledge and policy transfer. These managers are also 'policy entrepreneurs', in that they regularly reset the security bar, renewing their knowledge, technology and policy stocks, and stimulating change in other municipalities. MCS managers are thus vital brokers of knowledge among security communities. As the Ottawa job description puts it, the MCS manager oversees 'liaising with representatives of municipal, provincial and federal government agencies, professional associations, educational institutions, and the private sector, to initiate, develop and implement effective partnerships'. The MCS manager also 'stays abreast of government, business, industry, and market information that may reveal opportunities for new products and innovative approaches to service delivery'. Private security and insurance industry representatives could equally be called 'policy entrepreneurs', insofar as they are involved in establishing MCS as a security and insurance market.

Liability and Insurance

As noted previously, liability is a key concern that crosscuts the work of MCS. In the province of Ontario, '[a]ll municipalities have risk management policies to one degree or another and most large municipalities now employ risk managers precisely to ... limit liability exposure in the design of facilities, programs, and insurance coverage' (AMO, 2010: 5). The City of Toronto Corporate Security Policy states: 'the City of Toronto needs to be concerned with litigation'.

This concern for liability and litigation is being intensified due to shifts in the international insurance industry. There is an emphasis on self-insurance (Baker, 2010), which we argue is the second major influence leading to MCS incorporation and expansion in Canadian cities. The cost of liability insurance for Canadian municipalities increased with a liability 'crisis' in the late 1980s and broadly again immediately after 11 September 2001 (Insurance Representative 1). Non-profit reciprocal insurance exchanges such as the Municipal Insurance Association of British Columbia (MIABC) and Ontario Municipal Insurance Exchange in Ontario were introduced in the face of insurers' refusal to provide liability insurance to some municipalities. Currently, these domestic entities provide insurance to most municipalities in their jurisdiction, but are themselves subject to pressures from mostly international private reinsurers, which are firms that insure insurance companies (Insurance Representative 1), and which, after 11 September 2001, required renewed attention to security (Ericson and Doyle, 2004a). This 'new vigilance' was to be 'effected through surveillance technologies, security personnel, and circumspection' (Ericson and Doyle, 2004b: 272) and passed from reinsurers to primary insurance providers such as MIABC and OMEX to municipal governments (Insurance Representative 1). Exchanges make available sophisticated risk management knowledge, to help recognise and reduce liability exposure to member municipalities, hold workshops, seminars, 'webinars', and send member email alerts regarding liability trends (Insurance Representative 1; MIABC, 2004). Non-profit insurance exchanges and traditional private insurers encourage risk management by municipalities through various means and transfer risk knowledge to risk management departments (Insurance Representative 1), which then communicate it to MCS units.

This transfer happens too when primary insurers visit cities to conduct risk audits of select municipal facilities, which include examining existing physical security arrangements (Risk Manager 1). The results are then used to support or considerably refine MCS practices at these facilities. In large municipalities with deductibles in the millions of dollars, these municipalities sometimes hire risk mitigation companies that engage in similar auditing practices using ASIS assessment tools: "We've done some work for municipalities around examining their approach to security ... What are the specific risks that have been identified that security is supposed to address?" (Risk Mitigation 1).

Asset protection

MCS also introduces a corporate style of security governance to municipalities, based on management of risk. As Johnston and Shearing (2003, p.: 76) remark: 'Risk-based thinking is fundamental to the corporate mentality...' Private corporations sometimes appoint a 'corporate risk officer', whose job it is to make 'organizational encounters with risk formal, manageable, and routine, that is, governable' (Ericson, 2007, p.: 141), and MCS managers must now adopt a similar role. To govern risk, they must 'collect data on everything possible' (Ericson, 2007, p.: 146), hence the focus on surveys, inventory, and counting in MCS asset protection. Related to the governance of risk, MCS departments engage in asset protection, thus ensuring that expensive places and things that a city owns are safe (Aradau, 2010). Asset protection takes the shape of measuring, counting and checking all objects, as one way of preventing or investigating fraud and theft.

For instance, the City of Saskatoon barcodes all items over CDN$200 classified as 'high risk': 'assets that are attractive and easy to move. These include assets from the categories audiovisual, computer, photographic, communication, business, fire, and police equipment'. However, as noted in one document, the City of Saskatoon aims for acceptable risk, as 'absolute security is too costly ... The selection of security safeguards must be based on an analysis of threat and risk and supported by business needs'. Such assessments are made through 'an iterative process that involves steps to select, certify, accredit, maintain, monitor and adjust safeguards'. Halifax MCS personnel routinely 'take inventory of all … assets, tag and bar code them and enter them into an appropriate database with assignment to a specific supervisor for ongoing monitoring'. The purpose of tracking inventoried objects and supplies is to measure the effectiveness of asset protection strategies. There is an overlap between this insurance-driven protection and private security provision, as Stenning (2000: 344) remarks: 'Insurance contracts also commonly include minimum requirements for the policing and security of the properties being insured…'.

MCS departments elsewhere likewise keep inventories and protect assets. Vancouver MCS 'develops integrated security strategies for the long-term protection of City assets'. In Toronto, 'all losses of City assets due to theft, reported to the Insurance and Risk Management Unit, are investigated by Corporate Security and a Security Incident Report is created'. All activities and things in the municipality are recast in terms of liability. In Vancouver, even 'the technology in use is becoming a risk as it becomes outdated, unsupported and more prone to failure'. Such failures could invite lawsuits, which provided a rationale for Vancouver MCS to overhaul their camera surveillance technologies in all municipal buildings.

The discourse of urban 'threat'

The discourse of 'threat' is prevalent throughout private security industry promotions (see also Newburn, 2001) as well as liability and risk management communications (Johnston and Shearing, 2003: 77). We have found that the notion of threat has also entered planning documents and practices of MCS departments too. The City of Toronto (City of Toronto, 2009: 15) imagines transfer of 'City insurance loss reports, H and S reports, Security incident reports and Police incident statistics to be help [sic] determine the level of threats for different areas'. This document goes on to advise that: 'Most City of Toronto public facilities were built with open access and were never designed to be protected against the security threats and issues faced today' (2009: 21). Public buildings designed to be open (to the public) are now problematised, precisely because they are open to the public. As one MCS manager put it, "there is always a conflict … people want free flow but then it's a risk to security" (MCS Manager 2).

Efforts at securitisation are salient in the case of the Toronto report (FOI: 37), whereby existing missions are reinterpreted to imply that security provision and safety (obviously beyond public police departments) are major aims of municipal government (despite being the traditional purview of provincial and federal levels of government). A precautionary approach to eliminating 'threats' cuts across MCS practices, and not only in obvious protocols such as the Toronto MCS 'bomb threat' and 'lockdown' policies. A precautionary logic is a governing rationale that takes the emphasis on risk, especially to property, even further to presume worst case scenarios, and which is closely linked with growing uncertainty about the capacity of science and technology to manage risk (Ericson, 2007). In several locales we studied, municipal properties are divided into public zones, restricted zones, and security zones, suggestive of an approach that aims to bar access to zones deemed to engender urban threats (Jones and Newburn, 2006). However, these threats are typically amorphous in MCS documentation. This focus on threat, and the resultant securitisation of municipal property, is a new security imaginary for Canadian cities. It is accompanied by aggressive imagery more characteristic of military operations and of policing the US and Canadian frontier than openness of public urban places. Within Mississauga's municipal government, for example, area security managers are called 'SAMs' (Brown, 2007), a well-known military acronym for 'Surface to Air Missiles', and the reporting system for Edmonton's MCS team, who patrol the downtown for panhandlers and 'aggressive youth', is called POSSI. Once this new security imaginary arrives in a city, there must be efforts to translate it for other departments and agencies in the security network, including city councils and community and business organisations that wish to hold events in public spaces.

'Threat' manifests itself in the mandate and mission of MCS. MCS conducts 'threat assessments' prior to large public events or the arrival of travelling diplomats and dignitaries. Tools to complete these threat and risk assessments tend to come from ASIS International. These assessments are shared with other policing and security nodes. One example of a threat assessment concerns a visit from the Mayor of Beijing to the opening of the ceremonial gate in Ottawa's Chinatown in October 2008. The threat assessment states that 200 important persons would be in attendance. The MCS mission for security at the event is 'to ensure the event is secure, not interrupted, provide plain clothes security presence throughout the crowd, maintain control of audience ... and to minimise any risk of embarrassment to the City'. The author of this threat assessment reports that 'the largest concern at this time involves people attempting to embarrass either the delegation or the Mayor. Attention should be directed toward ensuring no signs, banners, etc. other than those directly related to the event are present'. MCS leads the team, even though members of Ottawa Police Service (OPS) and private security are deployed in plain clothes and in uniform. Finally, the document suggests that there is: 'no threat at this time. OPS advises that Falun Gong has stated they have no intention of interrupting the proceedings. No indication of other threat at this time'. Falun Gong is a pacifist group, with no recorded history of incidents involving violence in Canada. The discursive positioning of Falun Gong as a 'threat' not only suggests the extent to which knowledge frameworks from the private security industry have permeated MCS, but also how MCS is engaged in policing related to Internationally Protected People, a task in Canada usually reserved for the federal Royal Canadian Mounted Police.

Beyond remote threats (for example, urban terrorism – see Graham, 2010) that may be animating MCS threat assessments (see also Walby and Lippert, 2013), there is also a focus on more mundane issues related to order maintenance that would usually fall to public police or private security:

• In Toronto, MCS personnel are to be involved in responding 'to off-site burglar alarms in City vehicle[s] ... screening unauthorized persons/staff ... and remov[ing] undesirables and trespassers from City owned/operated properties' (FOI, 16).
• In Victoria, MCS implemented a card system for all employees, to 'limit public access to staff work areas, reducing the likelihood of theft and potential incidents with strangers...' (FOI, 7).
• In Calgary, a chief responsibility is to 'respond to claims for and against the City in a timely manner' (FOI, 16).
• In Ottawa, the focus on suspicious activity leads to MCS calls for City employees to be vigilant in the workplace: '[S]ecurity is a cooperative function. All employees have a responsibility to take ownership of their workspace. This includes wearing Photo ID cards in a visible location, challenging persons you do not recognise who enter your workspace and reporting any suspicious activity promptly.' Ottawa MCS also monitors surveillance cameras in urban parks, called PAV systems. PAV systems combine cameras, motion detection and loudspeakers. The justification for the PAV systems is to prevent vandalism and graffiti at city pools, splash pads and playgrounds, though the cameras now cover other areas (Lippert and Walby, 2012). When a motion detector in a park is tripped during night hours, the camera commences a live video feed to MCS personnel in the City Hall monitoring station. The MCS

personnel command the person in the park to cease their activity and leave the area. If no exit follows from what is dubbed the 'voice of God' in marketing materials (Dieser, 2007), MCS personnel and Ottawa Police converge on the scene.

- In Vancouver too, the risk assessment tools that MCS borrows from private industry are put to work in the securitisation of a public library. Public complaints about 'the homeless and drug takers/dealers' and 'street people in the stairwells' became the impetus for a risk assessment at the library. It sought to: identify 'assets' on the property (including 'personnel, structures, equipment and information'); determine 'threats present for each asset'; assess the 'likelihood of threats being carried out'; and review current security measures. Part of the risk assessment involved the MCS manager conducting surveillance around the property, including at neighbouring coffee shops. He recommended that area businesses add a mandatory minimum purchase, which 'may dissuade the undesirable element from using the location' and multiple entrances be 'gated' to prevent 'sleepers' from entering stairwells. Finally, the MCS manager commented on a 'dummy CCTV' [closed-circuit television] in a stairwell, and consonant with the theme of risk management, the 'possible liability issues associated with the dummy camera'.

The conduct of MCS officers is couched in the language of threat deterrence and high risk, but there is variation across cities and many examples appear more like mundane order maintenance. In Kitchener, corporate security guards might 'arrest, safely handcuff, and detain offenders for Waterloo Regional Police Service'. Part of the job description also entails dealing '…with individuals who quickly become agitated due to enforcement (for example, gang members, drug dealers/users, inebriated individuals and groups)'. Thus, the discourse of threat animates MCS protocol, yet the specific actions described in documents often have more to do with order maintenance than anti-terrorism. This suggests that some threats activating MCS securitisation and policing and leading to purchase of technologies (that is, security consumption) designed for anti-terrorism efforts elsewhere may be unjustified, raising questions about MCS accountability in policing and security networks.

Policing, securitisation and accountability

Hermer et al (2005: 23) define policing as 'any activity that is expressly designed and intended to establish and maintain (or enforce) a defined order within a community'. The work of MCS officers fits this definition of policing, insofar as MCS engages in surveillance of major public events, deals with order maintenance on municipal property, and enforces criminal law and municipal bylaws. Yet the work of MCS personnel is not reducible solely to policing, since MCS also engages in securitisation of municipal buildings and property, asset protection and risk management. Again, new knowledge and credentials from ASIS International animate much of this policing and securitisation.

MCS departments are hybrid agencies that elude definition as public or private. They blur the line between policing and securitisation, by targeting and engaging people, conduct, spaces and things ('assets'). The line between policing and securitisation has become indistinct in at least two ways:

- First, the security studies literature tends to focus on the regulation of spaces and objects, whereas the public policing literature tends to focus on the regulation of people. Yet MCS departments involve both practices: regulation of spaces/objects and regulation of people.
- Second, the work of Zedner (2007) emphasises the temporal axes of policing and securitisation: security happens prior to the event, while policing tends to be reactionary or post-event (but see also Ericson and Haggerty, 1997). Yet MCS practices involve pre- and post-event temporalities of regulation.

Public accountability

This overlap also raises doubts about the actual and potential public accountability of MCS. In simplest terms, accountability means being answerable to others for one's conduct. The accountability question in policing and security networks is complicated, because decision making and responsibility rarely involve one agency acting alone (Virta, 2002). Given that MCS is situated in a web of agencies, prospects of greater accountability are perhaps more complex than for other entities that are typically subject to official accountability safeguards, such as the public police (Valverde, 2010).

However, MCS perhaps has greater accountability than might initially be supposed. It is *to whom* MCS is accountable and *the nature* of this accountability that is vital. In principle, MCS practices are subject to the authority of city councillors and are accountable to the extent that councillors are kept aware of MCS practices. However, in our examination of municipal council meeting minutes in the cities for which this information was available, we found that MCS initiatives and expansion are rarely discussed in meetings. On the rare occasions when councillors did discuss initiatives, it occurred 'in camera' and away from public view.

In our analysis of city council minutes, we could locate only a few references to municipal council discussion of MCS. For instance, between 2010 and 2012, Vancouver MCS was undergoing an internal audit as part of a review of all municipal departments. We also found that Ottawa MCS carried out public consultations concerning the previously discussed PAV systems in parks with splash pads frequently used by parents with young children. The public consultations typically occurred with community associations and downtown revitalisation (usually business) groups, but not with average citizens and the denizens who are the potential targets of MCS surveillance.

The Ontario's Police Services Act (1990) and municipal oversight boards do not govern MCS activities. MCS departments are difficult to scrutinise from outside the network, much less unlock and enter. The frontiers of police and security accountability are certainly not expanding in ways that are scaled to the growth in new forms of security provision discussed here and in other chapters.

The overall opacity of MCS services in Canadian cities not only means that political authorities and citizens have little input into the direction of MCS practices; but it also means that the 'fourth estate' (the media) has limited influence too. We could find virtually no mainstream media coverage of MCS establishment or expansion. Provincial security regulations require minimal licensing and training of private security guards on contract with MCS. Yet, only in some provinces (for example, Ontario) would MCS 'in-house' security personnel in principle fall under the purview of provincial private security regulations.

Moreover, in one such provincial jurisdiction, MCS personnel remained unlicensed, because they were deemed to be exempt from these regulations by MCS management in one major city (MCS Manager 4). In another city, in the same province where personnel were licensed, a parallel MCS-run citizen procedure was established that routed public complaints to MCS management (MCS Manager 5), potentially circumventing the provincial licensing agency's oversight. We also found that personnel entering MCS positions are subject to basic checks that pertain to all employees, but once hired it is unclear how they are evaluated compared to other city workers. Public corporate security agents, like ambassadors, community support officers and conservation officers, then become freer to police and to secure (and unfairly to coerce and to discriminate) than they might otherwise be.

Industry self-regulation

Regarding accountability, there is also the possibility of industry self-regulation. This association with ASIS International (for example, the fact that MCS managers imagine themselves as part of this industry) may serve as one form of MCS accountability, albeit not to the public. For example, they must receive accreditation through ASIS International. The insurance contract with OMEX or with private insurers is a form of accountability too, as is civil liability (Stenning, 2000), though in both instances MCS would likely be implicated as part of the larger municipal corporation, rather than as a separate liability risk. These arrangements do not bode well for citizens to know or influence what MCS is planning or how MCS is policing and securitising their cities.

Corporate security form is creeping into higher levels of government too.

Other public corporate security

Investigating several federal Canadian government departments – including Public Safety Canada, Indigenous and Northern Affairs Canada, and Health Canada – we discovered how each securitises its operations, and the practices, risk management techniques, and information sharing involved (Walby et al, 2017). There are patterns in security practices, risk management techniques and cooperation with other agencies to solicit and manage information. While these security professionals share much with municipal and provincial corporate security counterparts, at the federal level, operations share a central goal: to secure and guard such information from persons challenging or threatening Canadian 'national interests' and 'national security'.

This focus on national security distinguishes corporate security personnel at the federal level in Canada from municipal or provincial corporate security counterparts. This effort involves security and surveillance practices, and networking across federal departments, which reveals how new corporate security frontiers are emerging in Canada. Though these federal personnel engage in practices similar to provincial and municipal counterparts, drawing on the same knowledge and seeking the same credentials from ASIS International, their federal level exposes them to laws and policies that are unique in the corporate security realm. Though corporate security counterparts at lower levels are not subject to these federal policies now, they could be in the future, as federal level corporate security continues to grow on this frontier.

Conclusions

We have charted the arrival and explored the practices of municipal corporate security departments in Canadian cities. The work of MCS reflects our understanding of frontier in multiple ways.

First, state and non-state begin to fuse in MCS on this frontier, as elements of the private security and insurance industries arrive to influence municipal and other levels of government. MCS seems to act with the minimal oversight and accountability more characteristic of private corporations than local democratic public institutions. This is fostered, in part, by the infusing of new knowledge and credentials from ASIS International, developed for private corporations but now being transferred into new public frontiers. A rapprochement among literatures on security governance, security consumption, and risk and insurance is necessary, as no single literature can completely explain the establishment or practices of hybrid policing and security agencies like MCS units.

Second, these findings are only possible based on edgier or investigative methodological techniques such as FOI, since MCS tends to operate in a clandestine fashion.

Third, although there is less material regarding control of Indigenous people suggestive of the colonial sense of the frontier theme for corporate security, we would point out the corporate security team for what was called Indigenous and Northern Affairs Canada (INAC), but recently split into two departments, Crown-Indigenous Relations and Northern Affairs Canada and Indigenous Services Canada) lists secrecy, building and perimeter sweeps, identity cards, safety, and risk assessments as part of its mission, but not reconciliation, restorative justice or decolonisation.

MCS has arrived in Canadian cities via a convergence of the international private security industry, the international and domestic insurance industry, and other MCS personnel and departments already embedded in Canadian cities, which all amplify discourses of urban threat. To address these purported threats, MCS aspirations include securitising public urban space with new locks, barricades and surveillance technologies – practices that the critical urban geographer

Davis (1992) famously described 25 years ago in writing about Los Angeles as 'Fortress L.A.'. Since 11 September 2001, this securitising trend has dramatically accelerated on urban frontiers (Graham, 2010). Regarding New York, Zukin (2010: 156) remarks: 'Already by 2008, 30% of public space in the financial district ... was off-limits to the public for security reasons'.

Our analysis suggests that Canadian cities, and other cities where corporate security is taking hold such as in the US, are on the same trajectory. Our discussion of corporate security in the federal level of government in Canada suggests that this is happening on a broader scale in other levels of public government too. Here, a channel is carved out by powerful private security and insurance industries and is followed by MCS without much public knowledge, input or a governing logic that is necessarily consistent with the public good. MCS embeds itself in governments' workings, and transforms the material spaces and symbolic elements that form the urban frontiers in which we live.

Note

[1] FOI disclosures are available from K. Walby at k.walby@uwinnipeg.ca

SEVEN

Funding Frontiers: Public Policing, 'User Pays' Policing and Police Foundations

Introduction

Public police and security agencies in Western countries must be funded to operate. Such resources are required to pay for personnel and technologies. For decades, this funding is assumed to have come from state revenues, generated through taxes and dispersed by various levels of government. Rarely have public agencies been funded directly by private sources. For private corporate security units, the converse is also true: funding has traditionally come directly from the organisation of which they are a part, namely private corporations. These units do not receive public monies for their operations. Yet it is in the public realm where funding arrangements are adopting a different appearance on policing and security frontiers.

This chapter explores new and neglected funding frontiers of policing and security provision. First, we discuss what is aptly called 'user pays' policing and related funding arrangements (Ayling and Shearing, 2008; Lippert and Walby, 2014). This is followed by a detailed account of several kinds of users and their understandings of these practices.

We next identify some emerging trouble on this frontier, as well as looking at how it is being problematised and governed. One source of trouble in the US, as well as a means of responding to problems stemming from these arrangements, has been the emergence of for-profit 'user pay' brokers. We call these brokers 'vampires' on the frontier, because they siphon off a percentage of the pay destined in some departments to public police, to cover their underlying costs.

We then explore an equally significant funding broker: the public police foundation (Walby et al, 2017). We elaborate on foundation practices in the US and Canada, and include a discussion about foundations and police museum narratives as they concern funding frontiers. To generate further insights about funding frontiers, we compare these developments in North America to the current funding context in the UK. The chapter concludes by raising questions about 'user pays' and foundation arrangements for public accountability and transparency in Western countries.

'User pays' policing: tollbooths on the funding frontier

Many police departments in North America and beyond now offer 'user pays' public policing. This kind of policing is happening in Canada, the US, as well as in Australia (Robertson, 2013) and the UK (Barrett, 2016). Despite scholarship about it, and related arrangements discussed in this chapter, 'user pays' classifies perhaps more as a wholly neglected funding frontier than a historically new one.

Thus, Williams (2008: 195) has documented in his historical account 'constables for hire' in the UK, the almost never mentioned work of public police at theatres. This work included that of the famous London Metropolitan Police and which led who received to extra pay to the department and its officers in 1857. In several UK counties, he argues further, between 1880 and 1881, 12% of officers in Durham, almost 15% of officers in Glamorganshire, and 16% in Monmouthshire were paid through private means (Williams, 2008: 196). This is mostly a lost history, but it suggests that we may be returning to similar arrangements on the current funding frontier. However, the prevailing assumption remains that public police organisations have been funded by public sources for most of the 20th and into the 21st century in Western countries.

The premise of 'user pays', as its name suggests, is that the public should not pay for private use of the public police. Those who use their security services for private benefit should pay, and the more they use them, the more they should pay. In practice, this involves selling security services to individuals and organisations for street festivals, funeral escorts, concerts, special parades and retail establishments, and sometimes directly to private security firms themselves (see Table 7.1). These arrangements always entail uniformed officers providing security to these 'users' via temporary assignment.

Our research shows that 'user pays' funding arrangements involving corporate and other mostly private entities are evident across North America. A wide variety of users pay the toll to secure a public police presence for their interests, as Table 7.1 shows regarding 18 North American police departments.

The notion of 'user pays' is obvious within private corporations or public organisations, such as those tasked with airport security passenger screening (Lippert and O'Connor, 2003), which contract with a private firm to provide security personnel for public security reasons. It is less

Table 7.1 Organisation/event type for paid assignments in 18* police departments, 2015

Type of organisation or event	Number of assignments	Percentage of assignments
Construction/transportation company	3,735	21.3
Special event/parade	1,599	9.1
Shopping centre/mall/store	1,322	7.5
Electrical/utilities/engineering company	1,231	7.0
Sporting event	1,139	6.5
TV/film production	1,102	6.3
City/municipality	927	5.3
Security company	724	4.1
Religious institution	541	3.1
Parking garage/lot	522	3.0
Funeral home	504	2.9
Bar/nightclub	480	2.7
Jail/detention centre	455	2.6
School	454	2.6
Social service	433	2.5
University/college	347	2.0
Concert/music festival	292	1.7
Court services	292	1.7
Real estate	197	1.1
Community club	181	1.0
Others**	1,038	6.0
Total assignments	**17,515**	**100.0**

*Department 2015 data from Hamilton, Detroit, York Region (Ontario), Seattle, Regina, Vancouver, Quebec City, Calgary, Peterborough, Surrey (British Columbia), Guelph, Thunder Bay, Saanich, Sault Ste. Marie, Woodstock, Longueuil, Red Deer, and Orangeville. **These 14 types of organisation/event each comprised less than 1% of assignments.

evident when the services are being provided by public organisations like the public police. On funding frontiers, whether it is appropriate to conceive of public police presence as merely a service to be 'used' by whoever can pay seems rarely to enter the equation. A different kind of mathematics is being used. Here, funding arrangements become murkier, less defined, more variable, and, as we discuss later, can cause trouble.

This variability is reflected by the numerous terms used for these 'user pays' arrangements across Canadian and US jurisdictions. Canadian police departments characterise this service as 'special duty' or 'paid duty' and sometimes under a larger umbrella of 'charge-back', whereas state police departments in the US call it 'paid detail' (as in New York City) or 'off-duty' security-related employment (as in Cleveland). Regardless of the term, all officers receive extra pay to provide these services in addition to regular on-duty police salaries.

This results in significantly higher salaries and is often lucrative for the officers involved. The average addition to regular officer salaries in one regional police department was CDN$6,000 according to one police administrator (Police Representative 5). This varied widely across officers, with some making many times more than that in some departments. For example, in Cincinnati, Ohio, seven officers, by adding to regular salaries, made more than US$200,000 due to 'paid detail' assignments, with one officer only US$2,000 shy of US$300,000 from April 2016 to April 2017 (Enquirer, 2017).

The extent of 'user pays' policing in North America is significant. A recent US survey of non-federal police departments employing some 143,000 officers showed that 80% allow officers to engage in these extra security-related private assignments (Stoughton, 2017: 1847). One ex-police officer, who oversees these assignments in one of the largest US states, remarked on their prevalence:

> 'It's very common pretty much throughout the state that … the vast majority of police officers who work for cities and counties and even some state agencies work … on what they'd call an extra job or an off duty police service assignment and what they do is they supplement their income by working with varying degrees of permission from their agencies depending on the agency … usually directly for private businesses or corporations in a highly industrialized area … There is … everything from churches to retail stores to office buildings to refineries it's *very, very*

common to hire an off duty police officer.' (Paid Detail Police Representative 1; emphasis added)

The number of assignments to mostly private users varies significantly across police departments, but this is indexed to a department's size. For example, in 2015, according to police logs obtained through our FOI requests:

- the large San Francisco police department (more than 1,500 officers) had almost 11,000 assignments;
- the mid-sized police department in Hamilton, Canada (more than 650 officers) had more than 3,500 assignments;
- the tiny Saanich Police in Canada (with only 45 officers) had only 22 assignments that year.

One major user of 'paid detail' services is the private retail sector, including business improvement districts (BIDs), discussed in Chapter Five. Although there may be a trend towards 'clean and safe' security arrangements in many BIDs (see Chapter Five), public police presence is sometimes preferred to be purchased over hiring ambassadors. As a member of a BID umbrella organisation related, compared to cheaper ambassadors or private security guards, the public police are deemed to provide 'actual policing':

> 'That's ... some of the BIDs' opinion of security companies. They're not trained the same way as an officer and they don't ... have that sort of respect ... They're great ... at night-time. Here we have a problem because you might have graffiti and small things in the downtown core ... certainly a police officer is not going to patrol watching people spray [paint] the building ... It might behove us to have a small security company ... and that may be effective in giving us information, but it's a far cry from I think *actual policing.*' (BID Umbrella Organisation; emphasis added)

This suggests, too, why various organisations – not only BIDs – want to hire public police for security provision. But this 'actual policing' can be expensive and often costs much more than ambassadors and private security guards. In a few BIDs in Canada, especially, security enhancement is nonetheless provided by public police through 'user pays' arrangements:

'One of the members of the board said "... increase the security on the street". From that point forward I started negotiating with the police department. We worked out a schedule and costs and we hired police officers who walked on foot patrols ... The point was we wanted to have a police *presence* right on the street.' (BID Coordinator 1; emphasis added)

Many users shared this preference for public police to provide a presence for security purposes. Officers rarely serve as knowledge workers. Their presence helps to manage private and public risk and is typically what is being purchased by private entities:

'...for us as a school in terms of risk management and liability ... then that's working to our benefit because we place them at the spots where a police *presence* is better for the students ... crossing the street, but then also with the visual presence to the drivers just within City. They see there's a police officer so they're ... paying attention ... the risk management and the liability factor is a bonus as well, in terms of peace of mind.' (User 4; emphasis added)

'Paid detail' police are therefore present outside a business directing traffic, but they are not expected to investigate, charge or wield criminal law when on 'paid detail'. Paid detail police are often expected to deter through their presence alone (Lippert et al, 2016); they rarely make arrests or lay charges or even issue traffic tickets. This means that 'paid detail' often entails – and appears to onlookers to involve – public police simply waiting around for long periods of time. This and other aspects can lead to trouble on this frontier.

Troubles on funding frontiers

In several police departments, controversy has emerged regarding 'user pays' policing. In Toronto, the high cost of these 'user paid' services, especially when charged to other City of Toronto departments, has been problematised (Lippert and Walby, 2014). This has been partially due to the high visibility of the same one or two uniformed officers standing around road construction sites, guarding excavations throughout the city. The stationary or inactive nature of this work – the fact that it entails simply waiting around, since almost the sole focus is being present, and that their pace and tempo is even slower than that of community safety officer (CSO) work noted earlier – has caused problems. Here, the dawdling pace of 'paid detail' work has been problematised, their extremely slow pace and tempo becoming a source of criticism and deemed wasteful (Lippert and Walby, 2014), rather than being seen to reassure, as with CSOs. This led to curtailing of these assignments and replacing the ones for traffic duty with much less expensive construction personnel who direct traffic using signs and flags.

In other sites in Canada, as a response to troubles (albeit not full-blown evidence of corruption as discussed later), an assignment procedure that uses randomisation to deploy officers interested in carrying out the assignment was introduced. This is a way of avoiding personal relationships between officers and employers since there is no way of knowing which officer will be assigned to a given 'paid detail' assignment in each instance. In Windsor, Ontario this arrangement was implemented following concerns about cash being paid directly to officers at the end of the night, the potential of looking the other way, and officers 'owning' sites that they would return to each week (Lippert, 2007).

There is a general trend towards more regulation of 'user pays' policing in North American public police departments, for example in Gary, Indiana (Post–Tribune, 2015). There and elsewhere this has been due to the optics that police being hired were – or could be – 'looking the other way', rather than enforcing the law. Police administrators are increasingly aware of what their officers might do, have done, or risk having done to them, in users' private spaces far beyond police administrators' oversight and remit on the frontier. Thus, officers' forays into mostly private sites and events that are so lucrative come with moral and physical risks to officers – and ultimately to the police department.

But in the two cases of Seattle and Jersey City, 'user pays' policing has recently become associated with full-blown corruption – decidedly more serious trouble on the frontier. This trouble has ironically activated the public police to respond at taxpayer expense – in this case, the Federal Bureau of Investigation (FBI).

Case study: Seattle

The FBI investigation of Seattle's off-duty 'user pays' system was sparked by public complaints (Pulkkinen, 2017) to the police chief about 'user pays' price-fixing, overcharging and racketeering, and by a police department audit that led a department representative to admit "that the lack of control of off-duty hours was a growing problem"

(Mynorthwest.com, 2017). One veteran Seattle officer allegedly bragged: "we would really break some bones if those (jobs) were messed with. Those jobs are a minimum of four hours (billed) and most are done in an hour and a half" (Mynorthwest.com, 2017).

The investigation involved several issues (Lewis, 2017), including:

- unchecked use of off-duty cops for high-priced security and traffic control work, after local businesses complained about being pressured to use officers or face unspecified repercussions;
- police and police-staffed security firms using strong-arm tactics to secure off-duty work contracts;
- overcharging;
- requiring 'management fees' to be paid to senior police officers, to ensure staffing;
- having no system to adequately track and oversee officers' off-duty hours;
- pressuring building and construction site managers to hire only off-duty cops to ensure that a police response arrives in an emergency.

These issues had been occurring for years. One memo noted that one officer proudly called his fellow officers a 'mini Mafia', in how they arranged, enforced and collected contracts. This officer admitted to overcharging by 'Seattle's Finest', a private firm (and an example of a 'vampire' broker, discussed later in this chapter) and 'squeezing' building owners, since 'no one in town has the power to stop any of it' (Lewis, 2017). Upon the FBI seizing the document outlining what this officer said, the officer related to the *Seattle Times* that he had used 'exaggerated, joking language for show', denying reports about what he said. But according to this officer, other officers earned US$1,200–1,500 a month without working a single off-duty shift.

Seattle's Mayor issued an Executive Order in September 2017, entitled 'Reforming Secondary Employment at the Seattle Police Department'. It states that Seattle's Police Department (SPD):

> does not directly regulate any secondary employers and has insufficient access to secondary employment schedules of off-duty officers, creating significant potential for mismanagement, conflicts of interest, inequities between officers competing for secondary employment opportunities, and which processes lack transparency to SPD management and the public.

Unlike Canadian and some US police departments, Seattle's police department was not in charge of administering, authorising and organising off-duty work. Instead, two 'vampire' companies had arranged this work for 'the past 20 years' (Mynorthwest.com, 2017). However, the website of one of these firms now displays the message: 'We will no longer be supplying off duty officers as of January 31, 2018. We are transferring all business to Seattle's Finest.'

The Mayor ordered city management of all SPD secondary employment: 'The Seattle Information Technology Department, shall establish an internal office, directed and staffed by civilians, to manage the secondary employment of its employees' (Jaywork, 2017. This is a situation as in Canadian departments, many of which have an internal office handling paid detail requests and deployments. The Mayor remarked:

> We will not let the private interests of a few police officers tarnish our entire police department … we need total overhaul of how this city handles the practice of police officers taking secondary jobs … Bringing the management of SPD secondary employment in-house is both in line with national best practices and consistent with recommendations from City Auditor, the Director of the Office of Police Accountability, and the federal monitor (Jaywork, 2017).

As such, the Mayor announced that he would end the practice of private companies controlling the moonlighting of police, while calling for a task force to restructure how the police force manages those hours.

Case study: Jersey City

Something similar happened in Jersey City, New Jersey. News reports on the FBI investigation of New Jersey City's 'off-duty' programme suggests it began around 2015 and escalated in 2017, when news reports proliferated. One journalist called the investigation 'an open secret for months' (McDonald, 2017a). The most commonly identified issues relate to bribery and conspiracy to commit fraud (Department of Justice, US Attorney's Office, 2017), and to 'accept corrupt payments' (McDonald, 2017b). Issues here included bribery, conspiracy to commit fraud (Department of Justice, US Attorney's Office, 2017) and acceptance of corrupt payments (McDonald, 2017b). Several officers were identified:

- First, the previous job coordinator for one precinct started his scheme in 2009. This officer's scheme involved telling private companies and individuals to contact him rather than the City to arrange off-duty work. As such, he became the broker. He then authorised these users to pay him or other officers in the scheme. Sometimes the officer(s) took full payments for jobs, but other times he offered users discounts, to entice them to contact him first for other future events. He authorised users to perform events unsupervised by officers and is reported to have collected over US$230,000 from users (Heinis, 2016; McDonald, 2017a).

- The assistant job coordinator from 2008 to 2016 of another district was involved too. One reporter explained that he 'assigned police officers to off-duty details [and] provided fraudulent off-duty employment vouchers to another police officer "identified in the information as Co-Conspirator 1"' (McDonald, 2017b). The officer reportedly accepted money from the City rather than from users for work that he never performed but still tallied on his hours sheet. He also aided another officer to do similar acts. The officer pleaded guilty to a bribery conspiracy related to the off-duty jobs programme, and admitted to one count of conspiracy to commit fraud and accept corrupt payments.

- A third police official, the former Jersey City Chief, also admitted to defrauding the Jersey City Housing Authority (JCHA), by obtaining compensation for off-duty work he did not perform (Department of Justice, US Attorney's Office, 2018). He admitted submitting time sheets representing certain security shifts, even though he was not present and was paid a total of US$31,713 for work not performed. Between 2010 and 2014, the JCHA had hired Jersey City police officers to provide security at some housing sites. The former Chief pleaded guilty to embezzling, stealing, obtaining by fraud, misapplying, and without authority converting money belonging to the JCHA. He is facing a maximum penalty of 10 years (others typically facing up to five years) in prison and a US$250,000 fine.

- Three other officers participated in a bribery scheme through which they had acquired thousands of dollars. All face imprisonment and a US$250,000 fine (McDonald, 2017d).

Noteworthy during ongoing FBI investigations was the Mayor of Jersey City's message posted on Twitter, stating that he would end the off-duty programme and that '[f]or too long the program has been abused with police officers more focused on off-duty work than on-duty work' (McDonald, 2017c). The tweet came following sentencing of one of the officers charged in the FBI investigation. Apparently, 10 minutes after the Mayor's tweet, over 40 'angry cops' called City officials to express concern. One police officer stated in response to the Mayor's announcement:

> 'We'd much prefer to have this conversation with [the Mayor] face-to-face than through social media or the press. While we understand the need for change in the way assignments are distributed, we hope that he understands how critically important these jobs are.'

Jersey City may now be 'revamping' the off-duty programme, according to some reports, but it may be ended altogether too (McDonald, 2017b). A retired NYPD Deputy Chief of Police also commented on the situation, suggesting that they should 'mimic how these jobs are handled in New York City' (McDonald, 2017c). In 2018, the Mayor announced at City Hall that the City is dismantling the programme and will:

> 'suspend immediately the requirement for off-duty cops for jobs that involve private citizens, truck and delivery escorts, jobs with businesses with liquor licenses, and for the Jersey City Housing Authority. Other off-duty assignments, like those at large construction sites and work by utility companies that involve traffic management, will end sometime in the next year.' (McDonald, 2018)

The Mayor remarked:

> 'We thought this program was corrupt in so many different facets that the only outcome that was acceptable to us and, we think, responsible for the Jersey City taxpayers, residents and for the future of the Jersey City Police Department is to end the program in its entirety.' (McDonald, 2018)

It was reported that in 2017, according to city payroll data, the 800 cops who worked off-duty jobs took in a total of US$16 million. The Mayor stated: 'When you have $16 million or $17 million per year running through this program, it's hard to keep it accountable [...] It's clearly hard to keep people honest' (News12 New Jersey, 2018).

There are other similar examples in US cities, including notably New Orleans. Such programmes might not just be slippery slopes to corruption (Coleman, 2004), but may be more like rollercoasters that take unwitting police, buyers and the public at large on a wild, sleazy ride.

'User pays' brokers – or 'vampires'

On the new funding frontiers, corruption is one major hazard. Another is the 'vampire', which has been around in the form of a broker as long as 'user pays' arrangements have been in place. We refer to 'vampires' in the Marxist sense of guzzling or 'sucking' value out of labour and circulation of capital. One might think of this type of agency as lying in wait to prey on these private–public exchanges and to 'suck' the 'life-blood' destined to public police to cover the costs of selecting, training and outfitting their officers in the first place.

In some US jurisdictions, these entities broker between users of public police services and the police agencies and officers themselves. This development is partially a function of legislation in the particular jurisdiction which permits this, but in Ohio and Texas, for example, there are private agencies emerging as brokers that siphon revenue from the public via the 'paid detail' process.

Besides the example of Seattle discussed earlier, another is Frizell Group International of Texas that claims to serve as a form of risk mitigation and a way for police departments to reduce administrative costs in providing 'off-duty police services'. This entity promises to:

> enhance the security needs of manufacturing plants, retail establishments, office buildings, banks, hospitals, and other facilities. This generally entails contacting one or more local police agencies … It can become complicated with multiple officers, multiple sites, shift issues, and availability issues. It can also become an administrative nightmare to pay each officer every one or two weeks and to prepare appropriate tax forms for each officer at the end of every year. (Frizell Group International, 2017)

Another 'vampire' organisation representative explains their sales pitch:

> [S]o they had off duty police and they hired them for years and years … but they began to realize that they were putting themselves at risk … and I'll tell you why … there's other companies that have been doing this longer than us but we started our off duty police services division and so what we

do is we go to businesses and say to them 'look you have been hiring off duty police officers for years and years a varying amount just depending on the client and you have spent big bags of money on doing so but you have fooled yourself into thinking that you have no risk or potential liability as a result of it'. So … if a bank directly hires an off duty police officer to sit in their lobby and a masked man welding an assault rifle comes busting through the doors of the bank and there is in fact a shoot out … even though the officer is off duty the very millisecond … in which he has to take law enforcement action even though he's off duty he instantly is on duty … so now he has all the rights, protection and coverage … of his agency and his law enforcement training and experience and all of that stuff and the municipality's immunity from litigation … so now he's in a shoot out with the bad guy and he kills the bad guy … let's say the officer is shot in the arm. He has a legitimate worker's comp claim which … would kick into effect because he was instantly on duty even though only moments before he was not. Well our speech to our clients is this that's swell if you have an armed gunman coming into your bank, but what if the chandelier in the lobby in the bank fell … and the glass broke and it took out that officer's eye you would be sued … because that guy or woman is not covered by worker's comp … so we tell these people look you put these cops in harms way just because … you put them in the same environment you have employees that you cover you're smart enough to cover with worker's comp[ensation] or in a …chemical plant … a chance of an 18 wheeler driving by and kicking up a piece of gravel and taking the guy's eye out. That's not so low so … don't hire the cops directly, come to us and here's what we'll do. We use costs plus formatting … it varies in different parts of the state depending on how many officers there are and the demand … but … the going rate is typically most cops will work for about $35 an hour … almost all of them have a four-hour minimum cause it's not worth them suiting up otherwise. Well we pay the cop the same $35 an hour … we don't keep a penny of that, so we would charge our client $35 an hour plus a fee … 30-35% of that fee we do … all the payroll so you don't have to write a 100 cheques next week if you had a 100 cops a week you only have to

> write one cheque a month ... we [also] take care of the 1099 [US Internal Revenue Service] fees at the end of the year say we have one client that single handedly uses 400 or more officers over the course of the year they don't have to do one ... we do it. (Off-duty Police Broker 1)

The introduction of this intermediary raises questions. Under these arrangements, users 'pay' the toll, but a sum is siphoned off to an entity not directly providing the policing, neither the officer nor the department. This phenomenon speaks to the amount of capital flowing through these 'user pay' tollbooths, and the capacity of some individuals (some of whom are former police officers, who know these channels intimately) to scoop value out of such flows. To suck up these pools of excess requires knowledge of police organisations, of insurance and human resources, and also a willingness to sidestep questions of criminal justice ethics and whether a profit should be turned from policing at all.

Police foundations: private encampments on the funding frontier

Public police in Canada and the US have begun establishing private foundations that arrange donations to fund police initiatives on the funding frontier. In Canada and the US, there are strict police department-level rules for direct private sponsorship of public police. One foundation representative compared firefighters' raising money by holding a big gumboot in public, to what police are permitted to do: "Police cannot stand there and take money ... So that's another reason for the foundation. Our police department under the Police Act ... can't do what firefighters do ... so their [police] charitable society can do much more." Foundations allow private funds to be channelled indirectly, circumventing these rules and Acts.

As with 'user pays' arrangements on the new funding frontier, not all police foundations are the same. There are both philanthropic and corporate ideal types. We are interested here in the latter foundations that adopt a corporate model to raise private funds primarily for public police equipment and programming, as well as promotions and museums. Indeed, this is precisely how such foundation representatives describe their mandate: "We have been driven by the need for pieces of equipment or the need by our police department" (Foundation Representative 1). There are several hundred of these foundations operating in the US and Canada. While New York is the most well known and successful of these foundations, there are many more in the US. Police departments in Canada now want to encourage foundations too.

Because they circumvent law and visibility, police foundations operate like 'domestic shell corporations' (Jancsics, 2017). These are created 'legal entities that cannot be traced back to their real owners' (Jancsics, 2017: 4) and thus mask who is benefiting from and orchestrating its actions. As official independent charities, these entities must disclose financial information to the Canadian and US revenue agencies. However, the private dimension allows much information about foundation activities to remain murky, as well as for the foundation to act as a go-between for private donors and public police. Donations and sponsorships can be filtered through these shell corporations, whereas similar funds passed directly to the police would raise questions about corruption or bias (Graycar and Jancsics, 2016). Operating with a different legal status, and with a board of directors comprising corporate CEOs, foundations broker relations between private sponsors or donors and the public sphere, buffering police agencies and their top brass from accusations of corruption.

The New York City Police Foundation is the first (commencing in 1973) and biggest foundation in the US. One aspect that makes it interesting is how its sponsors are changing. Based on an analysis of the foundation's print 'journal' since 1987, the first sponsors were wealthy individuals and corporations. However, in recent years not only have more corporations been funding it, but also more and more other corporate *foundations* have been funding the police foundation, which in turn funds the New York Police Department. These opaque foundation arrangements – and the identity of who is funding the police foundation – are becoming murkier rather than more transparent.

Police foundations in Canada

Based on information from the Canada Revenue Agency, the first police foundation was established as a charitable organisation in Vancouver in 1995, though Vancouver Police Foundation claims to have commenced operations in 1976. Edmonton Police Foundation was created in 2000, Delta Police Foundation in 2002 and Abbotsford Police Foundation in 2005. Calgary Police Foundation was formed in 2010 and received charitable status in 2011. Typical of other police foundations, Calgary Police Foundation Board of Directors comprises members from major corporations including Nexen (a transnational oil and gas company) and PricewaterhouseCoopers.

These police foundations continue to grow in number and annual budget:

- In 2015, total fundraising revenue for Vancouver Police Foundation was $8,198,426, with over $7 million in donations and total expenses of $1,147,417. These figures also suggest that the foundation is saving cash to spend later. One board member in another Western Canadian police foundation described this as building up a 'war chest' (Foundation Board representative 1), a militaristic term not inconsistent with one of this foundation's major purchases for the local police – a mobile military-like command unit.
- In 2012, total fundraising revenue for Calgary Police Foundation was $3,283,157, with over $3 million in donations and total expenses of $1,727,435. Calgary Police Service received $220,907. In 2014, total fundraising revenue for Calgary Police Foundation was $2,502,442, with over $2 million in donations and total expenses sitting at $1,788,385. Calgary Police Service received $400,000.

Foundations can direct donations and sponsorships in ways that the public police cannot. For example, in one year, Edmonton Police Foundation accepted donations from private companies such as Enbridge ($25,000) and Northlands ($10,000), as well as other $10,000 donations from provincially based companies. In 2014, Calgary Police Foundation embarked on a funding drive that secured large donations from energy companies in Calgary totalling more than $1 million.

Foundations also need to spend money to make money. In 2016, Vancouver Police Foundation spent $60,231 on advertising and $133,782 on fundraising. Calgary Police Foundation similarly spent $139,512 and $88,262 respectively. Edmonton Police Foundation spent $240,983 on fundraising alone. Each year, Edmonton Police Foundation hosts a police gala. A table of eight costs in the $2,000 range but donors contribute even more. They also gain access to police decision makers at the event. One police foundation's representative indicated: 'We're doing a joint professional sports team–police foundation in the fall ... and we expect this will bring in 5 to $600,000 as opposed to the 150 ... level that we have [been] normally getting from our annual gala' (Foundation Representative 2).

Like other police foundations, Vancouver's displays a corporate consciousness in how it raises funds through print and radio ads, fundraising dinners, galas, targeted corporate initiatives and targeted personal contacts. As one foundation representative bluntly stated: 'We just phoned up people that we thought had deep pockets ... and that's how we started' (Foundation Representative 1). He added that there was a new, more targeted approach: 'Now … we'll have to go and sit down … and try and convince different businesses, that we don't know, that are big … to be on board and be annual givers'.

As corporate police foundations operate more like domestic shell corporations (Jancsics, 2017), these funds are increasingly being directed towards police equipment or initiatives. Vancouver Police Foundation has been behind several major recent procurements for the Vancouver Police Department:

- In 2016, this foundation allocated $12,950 for special medical kits and $30,000 for binocular night vision devices.
- In 2015, it allocated $47,000 for a boat, engine and trailer for the Marine Unit, $40,797 for a canine-mounted video camera system, and $75,000 for enhanced video surveillance for its mobile command vehicle.
- In 2014, it allocated $24,000 for an aiming laser for the Emergency Response Team.
- In 2013, it allocated $7,000 to a Crime Alerts system that would update subscribers on crimes in specific neighbourhoods and $15,000 for the Vancouver Police Department Ceremonial Unit, which sends delegations to public events and police funerals.

Also in British Columbia, in 2013 Delta Police Foundation raised $120,000 for a mobile command unit, a satellite police station (complete with computer workstations and toilets) that coordinates video surveillance at public events (Mangelsdorf, 2013). In 2013, Edmonton Police Foundation raised $85,000 towards the purchase of police helicopters.

Some fundraising efforts of police foundations tend to more closely resemble the strategies of for-profit companies than public government agencies. In this way, fundraising is one aspect of the work of police foundations, where their activities appear corporate in nature. Vancouver Police Foundation is the most advanced foundation of its kind in Canada:

- In 2011, the Foundation partnered with the London Drugs chain, whose customers could donate to the Foundation or purchase a $20 'I Love Vancouver' t-shirt, with proceeds going to the Foundation (Marketwire Canada, 2011).
- More recently, London Drugs and Vancouver Police Foundation partnered on the Kops Shades for Kids Campaign. Aviator sunglasses

– 'a signature look inherently tied to police' – were sold for $20, with the $155,000 proceeds being given to the Foundation (Vancouver Police Foundation, 2014).

These fundraising techniques of police foundations are corporate in form, turning the idea of the police into a marketable device to capitalise on and make money from.

Controversy

There is trouble on this funding frontier as well. As with 'user pays' arrangements, police foundations in the US, such as those in Baltimore and Los Angeles, have become controversial or otherwise problematised by journalists and other critics (Walby et al, 2017). There is some suggestion that private corporations providing monies to these police departments through foundations have benefitted beyond merely positioning themselves as good corporate citizens (Walby et al, 2017). In Canada, as foundations are becoming entrenched, they have avoided similar attention; this is true of their relationship with police museums too.

A further irony emerges when we consider more closely only one corporation operating on these new funding frontiers – the oil and gas giant Nexen, which donates both to the Calgary Policy Foundation and to the main Royal Canadian Mounted Police (RCMP) 'Heritage Centre' discussed later. Here is a corporation now tied directly to police legitimacy through sponsorship that even a cursory scan of news media suggests is associated with nefarious and illegal conduct. For example, Nexen was charged in late 2017 with eight workplace offences related to the killing of two workers at its oil sands operations in Northern Alberta after initially blaming the workers for their own deaths (Globe and Mail, 2017), the trial for which has not yet concluded. In a separate incident Nexen was also charged with offences under the Alberta Environmental Protection and Enhancement Act (2000) by that Canadian province's regulator for a massive pipeline spill a year earlier in the same region, claimed to be 'one of the largest in provincial history' (Mertz, 2018). The corporate giant pleaded guilty to one charge under this Act and was also found guilty of violating the Migratory Birds Convention Act (1994) due to damage the spill caused to an area frequented by migratory birds (Environment and Climate Change Canada, 2018). In the last decade, Nexen has entered Equatorial Guinea, a country with a dictatorial regime and known for major human rights violations and rampant corruption, and is making monies available to this government allegedly in return for secure access to their huge oil reserves (Gardner, 2005).

This is a corporation that sponsors public police activities on a new funding frontier, but which is now closely associated in the media with homicide or manslaughter, severe environmental harm, corruption and human rights violations. There is no indication that the relationship between the public police and Nexen has been – or will be – terminated due to these acts. At what cost to public police legitimacy?

Taming the past frontier: funding for police museums

Private police foundations are increasingly being used to raise monies from private sector sponsors and donors to purchase technologies for public police and to fund new initiatives. However, foundations are also used to raise monies to help shape historical images and memories of specific public police agencies and – although never stated explicitly – to create and maintain legitimacy (Tyler, 2004). Without symbolic legitimacy, no public police department – regardless of physical resources for personnel and technologies – can operate effectively for long.

In the UK and Canada especially, the public police officer has become iconic and intermingled with national imagery. English Bobbies, with their distinctive headgear and having the confidence and relational skills that make carrying sidearms unnecessary, and the Royal Canadian Mounted Police in their red serge uniforms – depicted in more than 100 Hollywood films – conjure up images of the UK and Canada respectively. As with conservation officer efforts to shape and maintain national images in Ottawa and other national capitals (see Chapter Five), the public police officer needs to have their past created, nurtured and rendered legitimate. Where possible, they require a specific narrative to make sense of how they appear today. Yet believable historical narratives are expensive to create and maintain. Enter police museums and the private police foundations that make them possible.

Visiting police museums of four major North American police departments (Toronto, Ontario Provincial Police, Royal Canadian Mounted Police (RCMP), and Detroit) reveals that they are all funded not solely (or at all) by public dollars, but instead by police foundations. In visiting these major police museums and investigating their funding, one is struck by the extent to which they are funded by police foundations. One also becomes aware of absences in museum collections and the focus of the displays which, when given the funding sources, is not surprising. There are narrow histories on display and they are funded almost entirely by the Friends of the OPP Museum, Friends of the Mounted Police Heritage Centre, Detroit Police Foundation, and Toronto Police Museum & Discovery Centre (a registered charity like other foundations), many donors of which are unknown. The Friends of the OPP Museum is an especially closed club, in that to become a member one must be sponsored by a current member, the majority of whom are linked to the OPP as past personnel. Thus, a narrow range of people will be permitted to raise funding and then have input on how the OPP's history will be told. The museum displays and representations are similarly narrow in scope.

The police museum collections have several common features:

- First, they neither provide much information about the emergence nor celebrate community policing programs that emerged in the 1980s. Nor is there much if any recognition of the increasing diversity of their officer contingent.
- Second, there is no mention of relations with other agencies upon whom the public police rely, or who collect and transfer information (and with whom previous chapters have shown the public police are networked). For example, there is zero mention of CSOs, ambassadors or earlier contract private security. It is as though the police have always worked on their own to maintain order.
- Third, even the development of 'user pays' policing, which quietly re-emerged some 30 years ago, is absent. The emergence of 'user pays' is not unrelated to public funding cuts of officer salaries and the reduced capacity of the public police to provide services, such as escorting valuable loads on highways in Ontario and to perpetually low pay of officers in cities like Cleveland and Detroit, where they are expected to do perhaps too much with too little. Instead, one encounters historical accounts of technologies, individual actors and criminal cases solved.
- Fourth, the mostly dark history of policing of Indigenous peoples in rural or urban areas in Canada and the US, and policing of disadvantaged urban populations such as African-Americans in the US (Bass, 2001), is missing from these private, foundation-supported museums.

The RCMP's Heritage Centre museum

The RCMP's multimillion-dollar Heritage Centre museum (near its training academy in Regina, Saskatchewan) has funding provided through a foundation as well as specific corporate sponsors. For example, corporations like Nexen are promoted as key sponsors of, in this instance, the RCMP's famous 'musical ride' display in the Heritage Centre.

The Centre covers the widely celebrated 'Great March West' by the earlier North West Mounted Police (NWMP) that partially sought to control Indigenous peoples in Canada's West in the late 19th century. This is depicted as an endeavour which was just that, 'great', involving much hardship for a 'crack regiment' moving over the frontier, but not necessarily for Indigenous peoples who already lived on land in Canada's West and were then 'tamed' by the NWMP's arrival, in part by forcing them onto reserves. A new major exhibit at the Centre is called:

> Building Better Partnerships: The RCMP and Canada's First Peoples. This stunning exhibit explores the history of First Nations peoples and the Mounted Police. The displays highlight the partnerships created including the early relationship of NWMP Commissioner Macleod and Blackfoot Chief Crowfoot. We highlight the key role of Métis guides and scouts and the vital partnership with Inuit Special Constables in Canada's North. (RCMP, 2018a)

At least there is recognition of needed improvement (that is, 'better') in the new exhibit, but the notion that early relations can be characterised using the neoliberal term 'partnership' is historically inappropriate and peculiar indeed, reflecting the increasing corporatisation of public police via private foundations (Walby et al, 2017; also see O'Malley and Hutchinson, 2007).

In the Heritage Centre, we find little overlap with the unauthorised (and arguably more interesting) history of the RCMP (Brown and Brown, 1973). There is only passing mention of the NWMP (predecessor of the RCMP, renamed in 1920) role during the Winnipeg General Strike in one museum gallery as a 'challenge'. The NWMP at the Winnipeg General Strike in 1919 had used force against striking workers and killed two to put down the largest strike in Canadian history (involving some 30,000 people striking against terrible working conditions, soaring inflation and limited labour rights), and which was supposedly deemed potentially revolutionary at the time by Canada's federal government. This arrival of the RCMP occurred after most local Winnipeg Police officers had resigned or were fired for refusing to confront strikers, with whom they had sympathy. At that point, the RCMP joined more than a thousand 'special constables', yet another neglected type of policing and security agent, who were hired and paid by local Winnipeg business owners to form a network that mirrors some 'new' arrangements involving corporate security, ambassadors and even the CSOs discussed in this book.

Nor is there information on display about the RCMP's scandalous illegal activities, like burning down barns in Quebec, conducting break-ins, for example to steal membership lists of a Quebec political party, and opening Canadians' mail that would lead to the McDonald Royal Commission of Inquiry in 1977 (McDonald, 1979).

Nor is historical information displayed about the RCMP's role at the 1998 Asia-Pacific Economic Cooperation (APEC) meetings ('the APEC Affair'), held on the campus of the University of British Columbia. This involved the RCMP pepper spraying and illegally searching and detaining students without charge for protesting against the arrival of Indonesia's murderous dictator, Suharto, and violation of other constitutional rights of students and protestors to lawfully demonstrate, leading to the resignation of the federal Solicitor General and another major multi-year inquiry (Pue, 2000). Instead, one learns much about a 'march west' to help tame the frontier, the museum guide's timeline skipping the years 1919, 1977 and 1998 as inconsequential (RCMP, 2018b).

There is a display of standard RCMP modes of transport through the years – from snowmobiles to patrol cars to (of course) horses in the grand hall of the Centre. But there is no display of the infamous 'fruit machine' used by RCMP personnel to 'detect' gay men in the Canadian federal public service in the 1950s and 1960s, by examining their pupil dilation in response to viewing pornography and branding them security risks, which had detrimental effects on their lives (Kinsman, 1995).

Detroit Police Museum

One similarly notes Detroit Police Museum's displays of a lie detector machine and stunning motorcycles used for patrol in the early 20th century. (Motorcycles are standard, in all four museums discussed, adding a 'cool' factor, but displacing other possible displays due to limited space.)

But there is complete omission of the 1967 Detroit Riots (much less the now common label of 'Detroit Rebellion' for the same events) and the role of Detroit Police officers in sparking those infamous events via killing African-American residents. These events are only now fully re-entering public consciousness through popular culture, such as via the 2017 critically acclaimed film *Detroit*, but from which the city of

Detroit, due to the subsequent exodus of economic investment and affluent citizens, has never fully recovered.

Toronto Police Museum

In Toronto, the police museum features forensic equipment and technique displays as well as several about cases solved by Toronto Police. The police car display is sponsored by the Toronto Automobile Dealers Association, with their name engraved at the base. The display of police arm patches is similarly sponsored by a local towing company, Diamond Towing Limited, which previously held a contract with the police for towing services. The museum itself receives monies from the Toronto Police Foundation.

There is no display about the infamous 'bathhouse' raids in Toronto that targeted gay men, when on 'the night of Feb. 5, 1981 … police descended on four of Toronto's bathhouses and rounded up almost 300 men', charging 289 with 'being in' a house of prostitution. This action, which sparked protest the next day, saw Toronto police officers remove their badges, so they could not be identified (Thomas, 2011). Even though the Toronto Police Service learned from these events – and since then Toronto police officers have participated in Toronto's Pride Parade, which was sparked partially by these events – there is no mention in the museum of what were heavy-handed, unjustified overreach and oppression. The subsequent progressive change in police relations with Toronto's gay community might otherwise be highlighted as part of the historical account.

Ontario Provincial Police Museum

The peculiar narrative of the Ontario Provincial Police (OPP) Museum in Orillia, Ontario – perhaps the museum most widely promoted as a tourist attraction among the four discussed here – similarly is one that begins with displays about agreements with Indigenous peoples to provide policing, but not about the role of the OPP at Ipperwash, Ontario and the 1995 fatal shooting by an OPP sergeant of the unarmed Indigenous protestor Dudley George (Bryant, 2015). With other Indigenous people, George was protesting about land taken by the federal government during World War II for an army base near Lake Huron and people being forced onto a nearby reserve. George's death led to a provincial public inquiry, which concluded that the Canadian federal government was largely to blame for stealing the traditional land (Bryant, 2015).

In the same vein, the official guide for visitors entering the OPP Museum states that 'before the OPP' in 1865 there were 'two small border police forces, the Niagara River Frontier Police ... and Detroit River Frontier Police received salaries and uniforms from the (Ontario) provincial government' (OPP Museum, 2014: 2). Under the heading 'Northern and Southern Frontiers' we learn:

> In 1909, when the OPP was formed, the province of Ontario was dealing with the effects of growth and the resulting need for greater infrastructure ... Increased immigration and settlement was the experience both in the remote north and in the rural and urban areas in the south. (OPP Museum, 2014: 3)

There is no mention of Indigenous peoples on these OPP frontiers; they are not so much erased from the OPP's history as never even included in the first place.

Coupled with the efforts of police museum curators, often (in two of the four museums with direct police officer experience), here the official history is spun, preventing alternative or contested interpretations from entering the story. It is impossible to include all momentous events and developments in the history of an agency. But no mature modern institution (police and security agencies included) can prosper and improve without honest acknowledgement of some deeply troubling – sometimes bloody – deeds and practices, as part of how they travelled to where they are today. If it is true that '[e]ach individual display case highlights an important point of evolution in our development as a police organization', as the OPP Commissioner writes in his forward to the OPP Museum guide, there are surely other cases that show such problems were overcome by the police organisation, but which for now remain unseen and untold.

This lack of extended acknowledgement of these and other points noted earlier in this narrow 'story', which is a tale mostly of technology, individual bravery and ingenuity of police personnel, superior knowledge, and reactive practice that commences punishment for the criminal element in the local lock-up,[1] is not unrelated to how these museums are funded especially when they are funded by police-dominated foundations such as with the OPP museum.

The UK funding frontier

While there is evidence of the emergence of 'user pays' policing in the UK (Barrett, 2016), thus far there is no evidence that foundations have migrated to the UK (or other countries). However, there have been mutations that make the UK ripe for comparison with North American developments.

We noted in the book's introduction that public policing in the UK is characterised by austerity. Policing in the UK has been subject to new public management that inserts performance indicators into police work, resulting in civilianisation of policing when these measures are not attained. As noted in Chapter Three on community support officers, public policing in the UK has embraced new public management that uses performance indicators of police work, leading to civilianisation when required levels are measured and found wanting.

The general onset of new public management has had far-reaching effects that are not evident in North America (yet). A major move towards fiscal austerity and constraint (Barker and Crawford, 2013) and a 20% planned reduction of police department budgets was announced for the UK in 2010 (White, 2015). While this led to only one major arrangement between a police department and a transnational private security operation (Lincolnshire and G4S) (White, 2015), due to negative media attention, the window for privatisation 'closed' after two years (White, 2015). Yet, White writes in 2014 that 'there are already early signs that the police outsourcing window may open for a second time in the near future' (White, 2015: 296). This may still lead to some privatisation of public police services and shifting those responsibilities to large private corporations to undertake for profit at public expense.

Yet, based on our analysis in this and earlier chapters, there is a sense in which concern over 'privatisation' exclusively misses the point and is ignorant of what is occurring on policing and security frontiers. Many things are happening there outside 'privatisation' (away from media scrutiny that makes connections), as outlined earlier, ranging from the proliferation of ambassadors to corporatisation of public police agency structures, to some 'user pays' policing (such as West Yorkshire Police and Kent Police) (Barrett, 2016), albeit not yet including police foundations.

Conclusions

New and neglected forms of private influence across North America represent a new frontier of corporatised policing and security provision. Funds are being courted from the private sector and directed to public police agencies. This is no experiment in privatisation, but rather a relentless approach that bolsters corporate backing and the underpinning of police practices and the legitimacy of police pasts. Enrolling a corporation to collect funds for a police foundation shows how foundations broker police legitimacy. It also raises questions about policing mandates, policing styles and their relationship with the public good.

The frontier of private influence in policing varies by country, and perhaps the private and the corporate have burrowed deeper into North American public policing than so far in the UK and Europe. As Kristof (1959) noted, frontiers are spaces where legal controls are lax, and not guaranteed. Police foundations operate with minimal legal oversight. Charitable status laws here become more of a resource and justification to keep questionable monies destined for public police in the dark on new frontiers, than for ensuring transparency of these transfers. On the new funding frontiers for public police, these new approaches adjacent to public policing challenge existing rules for donations and sponsorship, and risk eroding the public base of policing in Canada.

Yet, with 'user pays' policing there is evidence of growing concern and more regulation, due to the need for public policing to intervene in some US police departments. These murky practices are becoming associated with organisational graft, collusion and full-blown corruption. Police operating in these channels are more than benign 'security vendors' (Ayling and Shearing, 2008). They are more like corporatised cliques. It follows that we do not see these developments as ways of 'lengthening the arm of the law' (Ayling et al, 2009), as the most extensive work on 'user pays' policing to date suggests. Funding frontiers are far more complex and fluid. They have entailed public police associating themselves with corporations involved in harmful and criminal acts in foundations and permitting arrangements that demand other public police to intervene due to criminal activity by police. All of this potentially undoes the public dimension of policing, and ironically runs quite contrary to what 'the law' has typically represented in North America and beyond.

Notes
[1]   The OPP Museum includes the 'Orillia Lock-Up' display (case 32).

EIGHT

Conclusion: Policing and Security Frontiers

This book has examined new frontiers of policing and security provision in the 21st century, by adopting three major themes. These are that

- criminology benefits from drawing on approaches and concepts from beyond its disciplinary borders;
- this foray beyond disciplinary borders demands cutting-edge methods, such as freedom of information (FOI) requests;
- types of policing and security provision migrate and mutate across jurisdictional boundaries.

To accomplish this study, the theme of frontier was invoked as, at once, a source of danger and a sought-after destination. The frontier is to be found ahead of formal spaces of control as well as ahead of its time. The frontier is indeterminable by borders and tradition, and can sometimes re-enact colonial relations, whether directed at Indigenous peoples or other disadvantaged groups. This book has explored this shifting and institutionally unsettled terrain of policing and security provision.

There are other frontiers of policing and security provision not covered in the preceding pages – in some ways, the most obvious being policing of migration, which is increasingly a topic of criminological study.[1] That topic exemplifies subjects of the preceding chapters that future work on policing and security must continue to examine. Work in this area has led to the development of concepts such as 'crimmigration' (Welch, 2012), which sees the overlap of public policing (and criminal law) and immigration law enforcement. The notion of frontier has much purchase here, where this form of policing and security provision impacts on millions of citizens and migrants. The notion of frontier widens the spatial and temporal scope of research – and its relations to borders – to the vast fields upon which migrants and supporters well beyond borders operate, live and resist.

By examining various phenomena in the preceding chapters, we have sought to analytically augment and explore the notion of frontier in criminology and other social sciences, by suggesting a threefold meaning: as the edge and realms beyond conventional policing and security thinking and practice; how these forms of policing and security are studied in ways beyond and across clear-cut disciplinary boundaries; and as continuing colonial control of Indigenous peoples. In this conclusion, we draw together interrelated insights pertaining to frontiers of policing and security provision, and reflect on six core subthemes derived from the preceding chapters:

- Frontiers of nuisance, space and time
- Aesthetics: cleaning up the frontier
- Public police relations and brokers on the frontier
- Law on policing and security frontiers
- Moving funding resources to the frontier
- Overseeing policing and security agents on the frontier
- Contested frontiers

Frontiers of nuisance, space and time

Downgrading or dismissing the standing of ambassadors, community support officers (CSOs), conservation officers, and corporate security personnel on policing and security frontiers relative to the heartland of public police and contract security guards would be easy. After all, public police (and sometimes security guards) actively respond to criminal and even terrorist acts, their perpetrators being identified, arrested and directed into criminal justice processes that lead to eventual punishment.

In comparison, many agents and programmes from preceding chapters target nuisance and minor rule violations, or merely deter these forms of conduct through their presence. The public police and contract security, and the relations between them, are plainly more significant, deserving of most attention.

Such a dismissal would be a mistake. Crawford (2009) contends that not all forms of policing and regulation are criminal justice oriented; some target nuisances or so-called anti-social behaviour in ways that require new techniques and powers. The common phrase 'just a nuisance' is misleading, since policing and security provision is often targeting disadvantaged people associated with nuisances as much as nuisance itself (Cooper, 2002). Each new or neglected policing and security agent does so. Indigenous people 'panhandling/begging' outside the retail store at the margin of the business improvement district (BID) are cajoled by ambassadors; marijuana-smoking hikers on the trail are ticketed by CSOs; the campsite of the 'sleeper' on the park's secluded riverbank is dismantled by conservation officers; the anonymous 'Post-it' note reminder to lock the filing cabinet next time is left by corporate security for the worker during a lunch break; and the inebriated nightclub patron walks a straight line home, due to nearby 'paid detail' police presence.

As argued by Lippert and Walby (2013), nuisance is a central target in urban realms and is often not experienced as 'just' a nuisance by complainants. We are not lending support to the now debunked 'broken windows' thesis (Harcourt, 2005), and its notion that to eliminate nuisances is to prevent crime. Often there is effort to curtail nuisance because it is interpreted as more than what it seems to represent: moral breakdown, incivility, antisocial conduct. Nuisance is similarly used as a pretext to disperse persons and to eliminate acts deemed, rightly or wrongly, as serious threats. Or it is used as a form of racism and clearly demonstrates the third meaning of frontier, as colonial targeting and control of Indigenous peoples.

Fisher (2013) argues that more attention to the varied temporalities of policing and security provision is required. Policing is not simply about territory (Herbert, 1997), but is about time, and the notion of frontier encapsulates this dimension of social control practices too. A theme through several chapters has been this temporal aspect, showing that frontiers are about space as conventionally conceived as well as time. This focus on the temporal geography of control is evinced most clearly in attention to nuisances. There is a sense in which nuisance does not exist during specific times, regardless of where it is encountered.

Time profoundly shapes how policing and security agents described in preceding chapters do their work. Ambassadors must work only to 9 pm or 11 pm in downtowns; police insist the spaces that ambassadors patrol then become far riskier and overtake the benefits of ambassador presence. Conservation officers work with specific temporalities in urban parks with national significance; their practices are both retributive (or focused on past acts) and risk- (or future-) oriented. Conservation officers are especially apt to remove people from national parks in the mornings, before throngs of federal bureaucrats descend upon Ottawa's downtown or during 'tourist times', such as the annual Tulip Festival. They do this only temporarily through dispersal (see Table 4.1) rather than banishment, which is to be permanent. CSOs in Western Canadian towns do not patrol off-street trails on bicycle or document graffiti at night. Corporate security personnel occupy spaces of government mostly during the day, when those they are concerned about, often government workers themselves, are nearby.

Temporality is about speed, tempo and pace (Griffiths et al, 2013). The notion of the police 'beat' (the set temporal and spatial paths of police patrols from the 19th century onward) perhaps best underscores the prescience and value of these aspects. While preceding chapters have not addressed these finer features of the temporal, future research into these and other policing and security frontiers ought to do so. The lack of focus on these aspects by police and security agents themselves might well be another feature that distinguishes these neglected and new forms and their logics from more traditional public police operations and measurement. Thus, the speed of response time to calls in urban areas by police has been the traditional measure of efficiency, if not effectiveness, regardless of crime rates or other measures. But that was to change with the development of community policing, and its longer-term, proactive, problem-solving orientation, as well as its comparatively plodding, low-speed bike and foot patrols, perhaps best evinced in the work of CSOs beyond the urban frontier. The even slower pace of ambassador patrols differs markedly from the imagined purposeful patrols (though perhaps not from the popular image of public police loafing in coffee shops) of public police, actively stopping to give downtown visitors information or to record something out of the ordinary. The public police 'beat' can be contrasted with those of agents and agencies described in preceding chapters. The conservation officer works differently, peculiarly shaped by paths of urban parks, but also beyond paths, where homeless people have sought to set up their homes out of sight and away from foot traffic. They have a fast pace on the smooth trails designed for visitors, and then a slow pace as officers proceed through heavy brush and rugged terrain to look for those they wish to disperse or, following a complaint, wait to see emerge from that terrain and then approach and issue a ticket.

So too must corporate security personnel match their 'beats' with the work and life of the corporate personnel whom they are paid to closely watch. Their tempo must be offset from the regular corporate workers, slightly ahead and after the working day, to be in a position to see workers access the organisation's corporate spaces with swipe cards (or similar) and then exit through the turnstiles. They can see who is working late and who is coming in early. They must watch during the standard lunch hour to see what has been left insecure on desks during a sweep, while other workers are eating in the cafeteria or beyond. Their pace must match their organisation's speeds – higher output during the day and in the fall months, slower at night and in the summer. When they go beyond their corporate organisation's walls to do surveillance of, for example, municipal land, their tempo and pace begins to match the work of other agents (for example CSOs and National Capital Commission officers), who regularly police those kinds of spaces.

Aesthetics: cleaning up the frontier

Ambassadors, corporate security personnel, CSOs and conservation officers are engaged in physical and social cleansing. The frontier justifies actions towards spaces and people. As Peršak (2016) notes, the regulation of the merely rude and the ugly has become a key motivating driver of governmental and policing activities. Agents work through logics of policing and security, one of which is aesthetics. The downtown must be clean as well as safe, and parks must be free of real and human 'garbage'. So too must the fronts of government buildings retain a clean image –dismissed employees accused of a corporate infraction are escorted out the backdoor by corporate security personnel and dispatched with little due process, using techniques often learned from ASIS International training. These policing and security personnel get their hands dirty as they clean up, because of their distance from state law, in ways that the public police, in principle, cannot due to their greater visibility.

The temporal aspect of the frontier is crucial again here. There is a sense in which conservation officers are motivated by the aim of conserving not only space but also the past for the nation in their work in the capital's parks. They clean up remnants deemed unbefitting Canada's wilderness, which the parks are meant to represent, and 'free' these spaces of homeless people and Indigenous people – then and now.

Similarly, new funding from proliferating foundations is used to create and sustain public police museums. There is a sense in which they, too, are cleaning up the frontier. For example, they omit the bloody 1967 urban riot in Detroit – the largest of the 20th century in the US until the 1992 Los Angeles riots – that saw Detroit police officers kill 14 African-American citizens and is thought to have sparked those bloody events with unjust entry and arrests. There is only a brief mention of the role of the North West Mounted Police (the NWMP, the RCMP's predecessor) during the Winnipeg General Strike in 1919, where they used force and killed two unarmed strikers to stop the largest strike in Canadian history (involving some 30,000 striking citizens) on behalf of business and the federal government. These are hardly minor events, but they are wholly inconvenient to those constructing narratives bent on creating a form of legitimacy of public police on the frontier.

Public police relations and brokers on the frontier

Relations between private agencies on policing and security frontiers and the public police are diverse, mutating – even peculiar. Sarre and Prenzler (2000) describe the many relationships between public police and private security (see also Shearing, 1992; Nalla and Hummer, 1999). While it is often assumed that the state directs these relationships, this is not always the case. Ambassadors act as 'eyes and ears' for the public police. Conservation officers and CSOs have similar relations with the police. For CSOs, public police welcome load sharing that permits them to retain prominence without needing to do all the work. Policing in the UK has been subject to new public management that inserts performance indicators into police work, resulting in civilianisation of policing when these measures are not attained. Yet, each type of personnel undertakes their own policing or security-oriented actions without police direction at times. Corporate security personnel may call in police when criminal charges are warranted, but often feel that their own expertise is superior (Walby et al, 2016), so avoid involving police when possible. In some ways, these agencies constitute a departure from traditional, law enforcement-oriented policing.

Yet in other ways, public police are increasingly embracing private, clandestine funders often hidden by police foundation practices. Private sector involvement with public police through foundations (and related sponsorship) is about installing new conduits for private capital to flow into public police operations. On frontiers, there is little evidence that these links are best seen as familial relations, as in an 'extended police family' (Johnston, 2003). There is not so much a familiar embrace of other agents as a reluctant tolerance – or indifference – by public police.

Sometimes there is outright disdain among the multiple agents. For example, public police sometimes do not think much of ambassadors, seeing them more as a potential problem rather than a solution to acquiring good street intelligence. Conversely, corporate security personnel often do not think much of public police as potential employees, since they are woefully bereft of new ASIS credentials. Corporate security units are no longer the last resting place of retired public police officers, equipped with knowledge of building cases for prosecution. Ex-police officers may instead be deemed risky to bring into a corporatised organisation that prefers to keep its secrets and its employees' indiscretions in-house (Walby and Lippert, 2015a).

Even 'user pays' relations create distance between public police officers and their departments, since while engaging in this work for 'users' there is little direct contact with departments, even though they wear police uniforms. Indeed, as in US police departments discussed previously, in Australia this lack of contact with departments leads, according to an Australian Police Integrity Commission report, to 'integrity risks and corruption hazards' (Robertson, 2013).

When one considers relations with public police, brokers of one kind or another are encountered on the frontier. Thus, the preceding chapters have elaborated on how BIDs, foundations, 'vampire' brokers, and even ASIS International all broker with public police or other key agents regarding security provision, vital information, monies and technologies of varying levels. The frontier, due to its murkiness and distances, requires brokers to make and maintain connections, to navigate these spaces as well as times in ways not necessary or otherwise prevalent in the present heartland of policing and security provision.

Law on policing and security frontiers

Following Kristof's (1959) lead, the introduction suggested that a frontier is without 'widely accepted laws'. Previous chapters have revealed that state law plays a similarly peculiar role on policing and security frontiers. In relation to ambassadors, law is oblique, distant, and an uncertain resource to coerce those encountered on the urban frontier. It never permits full use, since these agents are not assigned these powers, and this creates a somewhat precarious role for these agents.

In urban spaces, ambassadors encountering youths or homeless people vaguely refer to, and feign direct contact with, police and the criminal law. Sometimes, these agents are trained to invoke trespass law, to encourage disadvantaged people to move on from adjacent private property. Conservation officers patrolling parks away from the visibility that public police endure, wield discretion and work from a different rule book. With powers only of search and seizure, they are unable to arrest persons without the assistance of public police. Conservation officers are not quick to engage public police, precisely because, on a frontier, police are absent or too distant to assist, other than for criminal record and warrant checks about those they encounter on the ambiguous lands they patrol.

In a different way, corporate security operatives avoid drawing on state law for their legitimacy, even when working in government. Their credentials are not police academy training and being sworn in, but instead they have ASIS International credentials. Here, corporate personnel may merely use public police and criminal law to threaten, obliquely, the organisation's employees who are deemed to have gone astray. Often it is preferred not to involve police at all. CSOs use considerable discretion, when pulled into the orbit of public police. Some issue warnings and tickets, rather than charging people with possession of drugs, when they encounter them in spaces that public police cannot afford to patrol in person.

In the new funding frontiers of public police, law is peculiarly distant too. 'User pays' public police are present outside busy businesses, directing traffic or standing by, but they rarely investigate, charge or wield criminal law when paid by the shop or production company. They might deter merely through their presence, but it is rare for police on 'user pays' detail to follow through with criminal law or even to issue traffic tickets. Indeed, the recent trend towards more regulation of 'user pays' policing in North American police departments is due to a growing public sense in those sites that police may be 'looking the other way', rather than wielding criminal law, as would be expected of someone in uniform. Police departments, too, are increasingly cognisant of what their officers might do – or have done to them – in private spaces of the frontier far beyond their watch and remit. Police foundations similarly operate with minimal legal oversight.

Charitable status laws here become more a resource and justification to keep questionable monies destined for public police in the dark on new frontiers, rather than for ensuring transparency of such transfers. In some cases, both foundations and related private sponsorship, as well as 'user pays' arrangements, have become associated with serious harmful and criminal law violations by corporate sponsors or by public police personnel, which is indeed an unexpected relationship with law on the frontier.

Moving funding resources to the frontier

How resources arrive on frontiers has been another subtheme of this book. These resources are traditionally human and monetary in kind, and they arrive through peculiar channels that erase or penetrate boundaries and borders, for example between public and private realms. While these multiple agents are undoubtedly linked into networks that transfer resources, simply claiming this fact is not helpful in understanding funding arrangements. Research must investigate details of these arrangements – the special interconnections created and maintained and, indeed, sometimes dissolved due to trouble that arises.

There are also funding experiments occurring on the frontier away from forms of legal scrutiny. The example of foundations as shell corporations in North America – and to some degree 'user pays' brokers too – are legal loopholes that are being exploited. Through foundations, private monies in exchange for police legitimacy serve as fuel shovelled into the public police engine. Through 'vampire' brokers, private monies that should cover public police training, selection and other underlying costs paid by the public are instead going into private pockets, to brokers and officers alike. These arrangements, along with the movement of knowledge and credentials as resources into public governments from ASIS International (yet another broker), are extending beyond traditionally defined arrangements. These arrangements increasingly involve powerful private (often corporate) actors purchasing a public police presence via 'paid detail' or buying legitimacy from the public police by sponsoring police operations, sometimes indirectly through foundations in exchange for tax reductions characteristic of a charity.

Programmes and policies – and the ideas they encapsulate – also arrive on the frontier but are often slightly altered. Thus, for example: CSOs arrive on the scene in Western Canada from the UK; ambassadors have been diffused from the US to Canada and the UK and even to Germany and Japan; ASIS International credentials are spreading to public governments in more countries from the US; and foundations have moved from the US to Canada.

The frontiers differ in each instance, and so do the policies and programmes in slight ways in relation to local contingencies. It is the notion of frontier that befits this experimentation and adjustment regarding, for example, CSOs in small British Columbia towns and ambassadors on the streets of Nottingham in the UK.

Overseeing policing and security agents on the frontier

The idea of policing frontiers is not meant to refer to a veritable 'Wild West', in which new and expanding policing and security entities are unregulated. Policing and security organisations are diverse, meaning that local oversight and democratic input are necessities.

As Johnston (1988) reveals, and likewise in cases we examined, oversight and accountability varied, depending on the agent. Ambassadors are themselves targeted by 'clean and safe' even in terms of their own presentation of self. Corporate security personnel are required to have credentials to reduce risk of unprofessional conduct and to avoid association with, and the taint of, private security (Thumala et al, 2011).

Depending on the Canadian province, various ministries oversee the work of conservation officers, and in the nation's capital it is the federal National Capital Commission. CSOs are regulated by provincial agencies too. 'User pays' funding arrangements – but perhaps not foundations – have been targeted by public police both internally, with the development of new policies (Gary, Indiana, Seattle, Washington and Windsor, Ontario), and externally in the US at least with investigations by outside public police organisations like the FBI in Jersey City and Seattle.

The point here is that oversight comes in many guises. These should not be assumed to be ineffective because they neglect the now familiar public police board and similar accountability mechanisms. As Stenning (2000) has hinted, the fact that police and security agencies operate in networks provides an overlooked dimension of accountability. Merely because these agencies operate in, and constitute, policing and security frontiers does not mean that it is a 'Wild West', devoid of oversight. New forms of oversight may be created that target these agents, for instance for 'user pays' policing and police foundations, as these phenomena become more well known and problematised.

One form of oversight is the new 'vampire' brokers, who manage risk for private users of police departments and police departments themselves, but who also suck the sustenance from these arrangements. These are monies that could have been administered and monitored by the police department itself, to cover recruitment, training and even uniforms already paid for by public monies through, for example, a dedicated 'paid detail' office to manage assignments and to collect and transfer monies and pay, as in most departments in Canada.

Contested frontiers

There is a sense in which oversight is always about contestation between watchers and the watched. This brings us to another idea, with we wish to leave readers: namely, that policing and security frontiers are always contested.

Resistance comes from existing agents – public police – unwilling to embrace the arrival of new forms of policing and security provision (as with CSOs and ambassadors), seeing them as an affront to their interests or an annoyance, and seeking revisions to implementation plans. Even the Winnipeg Police in 1919 preferred to resist, rather than become implicated in the oppression of striking citizens that the North West Mounted Police was prepared to lead (see Chapter Seven).

Any discussion of networks presumes not only cooperation but also resistance between those comprising the network. Resistance also originates from those directly targeted by new and neglected forms of policing and security provision: for example the 'sleeper', who sets up camp in a more obscure area of the park after his temporary home has been destroyed by officers; the urban youths, who refuse to move on from where they hang out, despite subtle coercion from ambassadors; the corporate employee, who takes issue with being monitored after work hours by corporate security, and so on.

This contestation and resistance may well be another defining feature of frontiers, compared to established borders and boundaries. Frontiers are spaces where there is greater opportunity for revision and change. Therein lies potential for more progressive policing and security arrangements in space and time, and for more scope for future scholarship.

A final word

If policing and security provision can usefully be conceived in terms of frontiers, then so too can criminological inquiry. We hope that our foray into the frontier theme's multiple meanings – related to new and neglected agents and arrangements – are useful to future criminological work.

In 'The Last Resort' – the last song of their world-famous 1976 *Hotel California* album alluding to elimination of Indigenous peoples and destruction of 'paradise' at one continent's edge – The Eagles poignantly chanted: 'there is no more new frontier, we have got to make it here. We satisfy our endless needs and justify our bloody deeds. In the name of destiny.'

Policing and security frontiers are often driven by such private greed and entail bloody deeds justified with notions of destiny. But we think that new frontiers remain on our 21st-century horizons as places and times where and when progressive ideas and measures can migrate, animate and happen too – although only if violent pasts are acknowledged and begin to be righted into a future for a public good.

As we have suggested throughout this book, these ideas and measures might be animated not by destiny, deterrence and a preoccupation with a future plagued by unknowable risks to private property, but instead via notions of community, prevention, reconciliation, understanding, and public space and time. Criminologists can move that less determined process along, by opening doors to new concepts, venturing beyond disciplinary boundaries, and avoiding methodological pitfalls on the way to discerning what is happening on these frontiers, discovering and advocating for us what forms of security, politics and life are possible.

Note

[1]   Immigration policing agents, along with local public police and citizen volunteers operating on this immigration frontier, have received less attention than needed in many countries. As Decker et al (2009) examine, public police are becoming involved in immigration enforcement in new ways, but still consistent with the idea of borders more broadly becoming diffused in and across countries (Rumford, 2008). A recent ethnographic study (Armenta, 2017) explores the local public police in Nashville, Tennessee – far from any international border – and how their policing leads to risk of deportation after traffic stops for non-immigration enforcement. A related aspect of this frontier is how immigration enforcement activates a wide array of lower-level governmental officials working for municipalities and city governments that provide a range of services to people beyond local police. These people are to question legal status and report 'illegals' when they happen upon them and, in this instance, far from any international border. While immigration agents, such as the Department of Homeland Security (Walby and Lippert, 2015a), are most obvious, there are also US Border Control agents. We wish to make two points here. First, US Border Control agents, despite their moniker, work on a frontier. A longstanding provision from the US Immigration and Nationality Act 1953 as well as a related regulation allow these agents, without a warrant, to board and search for persons without legal status any vessel up to 100 miles from the administrative border. For this reason, these agents work far from the international line between countries, to seek out 'illegal' migrants, which has entailed boarding Amtrak trains headed to the border in, for example, Syracuse, New York (Dale, 2018). Another example of policing this frontier has not excluded Indigenous peoples in the relentless search for 'illegal' migrants and terrorists (Pratt, 2017). This is evident with the US–Canada 'shiprider' programme that permits US and Canadian border officials to patrol using the same boat to cover vast areas of an aquatic frontier between not merely Canada and the US, but also adjacent land lived upon, and waters used by, Indigenous peoples for centuries. While a one-sided arrangement in favour of US officials compared to Canadian officials (in that US officials enter Canadian territory to enforce US law, but the converse is not true) (Pratt, 2017: 260), policing agents of both nations become positioned against Indigenous people living nearby. The policing of this frontier has been a pretext to police residents of Akwesasne, Indigenous land that intersects and stretches beyond the Canada–US border (Pratt, 2017). In this way, Akwesasne has been increasingly policed as a zone of risk. The new 'ship-rider' programme to go after 'smuggling' through Akwesasne has not, however, gone unchallenged by Indigenous people (Pratt, 2017: 260).

References

Adler, P. and Adler, P. (2002) 'The reluctant respondent', in J. Gubrium and J. Holstein (eds) *Handbook of interview research*, Thousand Oaks, CA: Sage, 515–36.

Alberta Urban Municipalities Association (AUMA) Standing Committee on Community Infrastructure (2007) Meeting minutes, 9 November.

Alison, L., Snook, B. and Stein, K. (2001) 'Unobtrusive measurement: Using police information for forensic research', *Qualitative Research*, 1(2): 241–54.

Amoore, L. and de Goede, M. (2005) 'Governance, risk and dataveillance on the war on terror', *Crime, Law and Social Change*, 43(2): 149–73.

Amster, R. (2003) 'Patterns of exclusion: Sanitizing space, criminalizing homelessness', *Social Justice*, 30(1): 195–221.

Aradau, C. (2010) 'Security that matters: Critical infrastructure and objects of protection', *Security Dialogue*, 41(5): 491–514.

Aradau, C., Huysmans, J., Neal, A. and Voelkner, N. (2014) *Critical security methods: New frameworks for analysis*, London: Routledge.

Armenta, A. (2017) *Protect, serve, and deport: The rise of policing as immigration enforcement.* Oakland: University of California Press.

Association of Municipalities of Ontario Municipal Liability Reform Working Group (AMO) (2010) The case for joint and several liability reform in Ontario. Toronto: AMO.

Ayling, J., Grabosky, P. and Shearing, C. (2009) *Lengthening the arm of the law: Enhancing police resources in the 21st Century*, Cambridge: Cambridge University Press.

Ayling, J. and Shearing, C. (2008) 'Taking care of business: Public police as commercial security vendors', *Criminology and Criminal Justice*, 8(1): 27–50.

Bailey, J. (2003) 'Community safety officers... What do they do?', *Safer Communities*, 2(4): 29–32.

Baker, T. (2010) 'Insurance in sociolegal research', *Annual Review of Law and Social Science*, 6: 433–47.

Barker, A. and Crawford, A. (2013) 'Policing urban insecurities through visible patrols: Managing public expectations in times of fiscal restraint', in R. Lippert and K. Walby (eds) *Policing cities: Urban securitization and regulation in a 21st century world*, London: Routledge, 11–28.

Barrett, D. (2016) 'Revealed: Britain's privately-funded police force', *The Telegraph*, 3 January, https://www.telegraph.co.uk/news/uknews/law-and-order/12064205/Revealed-Britains-privately-funded-police-force.html

Bass, S. (2001) 'Policing space, policing race: Social control imperatives and police discretionary decisions', *Social Justice*, 28(1): 156–76.

Bay, J. (2016) 'Woman says NCC making vigil difficult', *Ottawa Sun*, 16 January.

Bazemore, G. and Griffiths, C. (2004) 'Police reform, restorative justice and restorative policing', *Police Practice and Research*, 4(4): 335–46.

Beckett, K. and Herbert, S. (2009) *Banished: the new social control in urban America*, Oxford: Oxford University Press.

Beckett, K. and Herbert, S. (2010) 'Penal boundaries: Banishment and the expansion of punishment', *Law & Social Inquiry*, 35(1): 1–38.

Belur, J. (2014) 'Status, gender, and geography: Power negotiations in police research', *Qualitative Research*, 14(2): 184–200.

Benz, A. and Fürst, D. (2002) 'Policy learning in regional networks', *European Urban and Regional Studies*, 9(1): 21–35.

Bergin, T. (2011) 'How and why do criminal justice public policies spread throughout the United States?', *Criminal Justice Policy Review*, 22(4): 403–21.

Besmier, M. (2003) 'Ottawa: Federal capital and first national symbol', *Queen's Quarterly*, 110(2): 197.

Bigo, D. (2005) 'Frontier controls in the European Union: Who is in control?', in D. Bigo and E. Guild (eds) *Controlling frontiers: Free movement into and within Europe*, Aldershot: Ashgate.

Bittner, E. (1967) 'The police on skid-row: a study of peace keeping', *American Sociological Review*, 32(5): 699–716.

Bittner, E. (1970) *The functions of the police in modern society*. Washington DC: National Institute of Mental Health.

Blee, K. M. (1998) 'White-knuckle research: Emotional dynamics in fieldwork with racist activists', *Qualitative Sociology*, 21(4): 381–99.

Blomley, N. (2003) 'Law, property and the geography of violence: The frontier, the survey and the grid', *Annals of the Association of American Geographers*, 93(1): 121–41.

Blomley, N. (2004) *Unsettling the city: Urban land and the politics of property*, New York: Routledge.

Blomley, N. (2005) 'The borrowed view: Privacy, propriety, and the entanglements of property', *Law & Social Inquiry*, 30(4): 617–61.

Blomley, N. (2007) 'Civil rights meet civil engineering: Urban public space and traffic logic', *Canadian Journal of Law and Society*, 22(2): 55–71.

Blomley, N. and Sommers, J. (1999) 'Mapping urban space: Governmentality and cartographic struggles in inner city Vancouver', in R. Smandych (ed.) *Governable places*, Brookfield, VT: Ashgate, 261–86.

Brady, M. and Lippert, R. (eds) (2016) *Governing practices: Neo-liberalism, governmentalities, and ethnographic imaginary*, Toronto: University of Toronto Press.

Brambilla, C. (2015) 'Exploring the critical potential of the borderscape concept', *Geopolitics*, 20(1): 14-34.

Braun, D. (2015) 'Goertzen wants community safety officer program available to Steinbach and Hanover', Steinbachonline.com, 12 November.

Brewer, J. (1990) 'Sensitivity as a problem in field research: A study of routine policing in Northern Ireland', *American Behavioral Scientist*, 33(5): 578–93.

Brodeur, J. (2010) *The policing web*, Oxford: University of Oxford Press.

Brogden, M. and Nijhar, P. (2005) *Community policing: National and international models and approaches*, Portland: Willan.

Brown, J. (2007) 'Shattering the myth of corporate security', *Canadian Security Magazine*, 17 February.

Brown, J. and Lippert, R. (2007) 'Private security's purchase: consumers' imaginings of a security patrol in a Canadian residential neighbourhood', *Canadian Journal of Criminology and Criminal Justice*, 49(5): 587–616.

Brown, A. (2017) 'City hiring another Community Safety Officer', *Battlefords Now*, 8 May.

Brown, L. (2016) 'Agency apologizes for shutting down kids' lemonade stand', *Toronto Star*, 4 July.

Brown, L. and Brown, C. (1973) *An unauthorized history of the RCMP*, James Lewis and Samuel.

Bryant, M. (2015) 'Twenty years after Dudley George's death, land still in federal hands', *Toronto Star*, 22 January.

Burr, J. and Reynolds, P. (2012) 'The wrong paradigm? Social research and the predicates of ethical scrutiny', *Research Ethics*, 6(4): 128–33.

Burris, S., Drahos, P. and Shearing, C. (2005) 'Nodal governance', *Australian Journal of Legal Philosophy*, 30: 30–58.

Cairns, J. (2014) North Battleford community safety model to expand province wide. *The Battlefords News-Optimist*, 3 December.

Canadian Broadcasting Corporation (CBC) (2015) 'Downtown Vancouver Ambassadors discriminated against homeless', www.cbc.ca/news/canada/british-columbia/downtown-vancouver-ambassadors-discriminated-against-homeless-1.3029392

Canadian Press (2016) 'Algonquin First Nation seeking land claim over Ottawa, Parliament Hill', *Global News Winnipeg*, 8 December.

Carrington, K., McIntosh, A. and Scott, J. (2010) 'Globalization, frontier masculinities and violence: Booze, blokes and brawls', *British Journal of Criminology*, 50(3): 393-413.

Carter, J. and Gore, M. (2013) 'Conservation officers: A force multiplier for homeland security', *Journal of Applied Security Research*, 8(3): 285–307.

Caruson, K. and MacManus, S. (2006) 'Mandates and management challenges in the trenches: An intergovernmental perspective on homeland security', *Public Administration Review*, 66(4): 522–36.

Chambliss, W. (1964) 'A sociological analysis of the law of vagrancy', *Social Problems*, 12(1): 67–77.

Cherney, A. (2004) 'Contingency and politics: The local government community safety officer role', *Criminology & Criminal Justice*, 4(2): 115–28.

Cherney, A. and Sutton, A. (2004) 'Aussie experience: Local government community safety officers and capacity building', *Safer Communities*, 3(3): 31–5.

Chunn, D. and Gavigan, S. (2004) 'Welfare Law, welfare fraud, and the moral regulation of the "Never Deserving" Poor', *Social & Legal Studies*, 13(2): 219–43.

City of Langford (2007a) Langford community safety and policing support UBCM community excellence award application.

City of Langford (2007b) City of Langford 2007 annual report.

City of Langford (2009) Langford community safety and policing support initiative summary.

City of Surrey (2008a) Crime reduction strategy annual report, 31 October.

City of Surrey (2008b) Crime reduction strategy—community safety officers, 15 September.

City of Surrey (2008c) Public safety committee minutes, 16 June.

City of Toronto (2009) City of Toronto city-wide corporate security policy.

Cockcroft, T. (2005) 'Using oral history to investigate police culture', *Qualitative Research*, 5(3): 365–84.

Coleman, R., Tombs, S. and Whyte, D. (2005) 'Capital, crime control, and statecraft in the entrepreneurial city', *Urban Studies*, 42(13): 2511–30.

Coleman, S. (2004) 'When police should say "no!" to gratuities', *Criminal Justice Ethics*, 23(1): 33–44.

Colley, T. (2007) 'More police coming in new Surrey budget; plan also include 10 community safety officers. Now [Surrey]. Community safety officers set to hit the streets', Maple Ridge, *Pitt Meadows Times*, 11 July.

Collins, R. (1979) *The credentialist society: An historical sociology of education and stratification*, New York: The Academic Press.

Cook, I. and Ward, K. (2012) 'Conferences, informational infrastructures and mobile policies: The process of getting Sweden "BID ready"', *European Urban and Regional Studies*, 19(2): 137–52.

Cooper, C., Anscombe, J., Avenell, J., McLean, F. and Morris, J. (2006) *A national evaluation of community support officers*. London, England: Home Office Research Study, 297.

Cooper, D. (2002) 'Far beyond "the early morning crowing of a farmyard cock" revisiting the place of nuisance within political and legal discourse', *Social & Legal Studies*, 11(1): 5–35.

Corbin, J. and Morse, J. (2003) 'Reciprocity and risks when dealing with sensitive topics', *Qualitative Inquiry*, 9(3): 335–54.

Crawford, A. (2006a) 'Networked governance and the post-regulatory state? Steering, rowing and anchoring the provision of policing and security', *Theoretical Criminology*, 10(4): 449–79.

Crawford, A. (2006b) 'Police and security as "club goods": the new enclosures?', in J. Wood and B. Dupont (eds) *Democracy, society, and the governance of security*, New York: Cambridge, 111–38.

Crawford, A. (2009) 'Governing through anti-social behaviour: Regulatory challenges to criminal justice', *British Journal of Criminology*, 49(6): 810–31.

Crawford, A. and Lister, S. (2004) 'The patchwork shape of reassurance policing in England and Wales: Integrated local security quilts or frayed, fragmented and fragile tangled webs?', *Policing: An International Journal of Police Strategies and Management*, 27(3): 413–30.

Dale, D. (2018) '"Are you a citizen?" To U.S. Border Patrol, the Canadian border is 100 miles wide', *Toronto Star*, 11 February.

Davis, M. (1992) *City of quartz: Excavating the future in Los Angeles*, New York: Vintage.

Decker, S., Lewis, P., Provine, D. and Varsanyi, M. (2009) 'On the frontier of local law enforcement: Local police and federal immigration law', in W. McDonald (ed.) *Immigration, crime and justice* (*Sociology of Crime, Law and Deviance*, Volume 13), Emerald Group Publishing, 261–76.

De Leon, J. and Cohen, J. (2005) 'Object and walking probes in ethnographic interviewing', *Field Methods*, 17(2): 200–4.

Dedicated Micros (2008) 'Dedicated micros helps to protect Canadian capital's pools, parks, and historic structures as part of proactive audio-video surveillance system', www.transvu.co.uk/ ottawa.htm.

Department of Justice, US Attorney's Office (2017) 'Jersey City police officer admits fraud involving off-duty work assignments', https://www.justice.gov/usao-nj/pr/jersey-city-police-officer-admits-fraud-involving-duty-work-assignments

Department of Justice, US Attorney's Office (2018) 'Former Jersey City Chief of Police admits fraud involving off-duty work assignments', https://www.justice.gov/usao-nj/pr/former-jersey-city-chief-police-admits-fraud-involving-duty-work-assignments

Deukmedjian, J. and de Lint, W. (2007) 'Community into intelligence: Resolving information uptake in the RCMP', *Policing and Society*, 17(3): 239–56.

DeVerteuil, G. (2006) 'The local state and homeless shelters: Beyond revanchism?', *Cities*, 23(2): 109–20.

DeVerteuil, G., May, J. and von Mahs, J. (2009) 'Complexity not collapse: Recasting the geographies of homelessness in a "punitive" age', *Progress in Human Geography*, 33(5): 646–66.

Dieser, D. (2007) 'City of Ottawa case study', *Pelco Press*. 17.

Doucet, A. and Mauthner, N. (2008) 'What can be known and how? Narrated subjects and the listening guide', *Qualitative Research*, 8(3): 399–409.

Dupont, B. (2004) 'Security in the age of networks', *Policing and Society*, 14(1): 76–91.

Dupont, B. (2015) 'Private security regimes: Conceptualizing the forces that shape the private delivery of security', *Theoretical Criminology*, 18(3): 263–81.

Earl, J. (2009) 'Information access and protest policing post-9/11: Studying the policing of the 2004 Republican National Convention', *American Behavioral Scientist*, 53(1): 44–60.

Edwards, A. and Hughes, G. (2008) 'Inventing community safety', in P. Carlen (ed.) *Imaginary penalities*, Devon: Willan, 64–83.

Edwards, A. and Hughes, G. (2011) 'Public safety regimes: Negotiated orders and political analysis in criminology', *Criminology & Criminal Justice*, 12(4): 433–58.

Edwards, A., Hughes, G. and Lord, N. (2013) 'Urban security in Europe: Translating a concept in public criminology', *European Journal of Criminology*, 10(3): 260–83.

Eick, V. (2003) 'New strategies of policing the poor: Berlin's neo-liberal security system', *Policing and Society*, 13(4): 365–79.

Eick, V. (2006) 'Preventive urban discipline: Rent-a-cops and neoliberal glocalization in Germany', *Social Justice*, 33(3): 66–84.

Environment and Climate Change Canada (2018) 'Nexen Energy ULC ordered to pay $290,000 fine for a violation of the Migratory Birds Convention Act, 1994', *Cision*, 13 July, www.newswire.ca/news-releases/nexen-energy-ulc-ordered-to-pay-290000-fine-for-a-violation-of-the-migratory-birds-convention-act-1994-688143551.html.

Ericson, R. (1981) *Making crime: A study of detective work*, Toronto: Butterworths.

Ericson, R. (2007) *Crime in an insecure world*, London: Polity Press.

Ericson, R. and Doyle, A. (2004a) 'Catastrophe risk, insurance and terrorism', *Economy and Society*, 33(2): 135–73.

Ericson, R. and Doyle, A. (2004b) *Uncertain business: Risk, insurance and the limits of knowledge*, Toronto: University of Toronto Press.

Ericson, R. and Haggerty, K. (1997) *Policing the risk society*, Toronto: University of Toronto Press.

Fielding, N. and Innes, M. (2006) 'Reassurance policing, community policing and measuring police performance', *Policing and Society*, 16(2): 127–45.

Fisher, K. (2013) 'Exploring the temporality in/of British counterterrorism law and law making', *Critical Studies on Terrorism*, 6(1): 50–72.

Foote, C. (1956) 'Vagrancy-type law and its administration', *University of Pennsylvania Law Review*, 104(5): 603–50.

Ford, R. (1999) 'Law's territory: A history of jurisdiction', *Michigan Law Review*, 97(4): 843–930.

Frizell Group International (2017) www.frizellgroup.com/police-services/

Frug, G. (2001) 'A legal history of cities', in N. Blomley and R. Ford (eds) *The legal geographies reader*, Oxford: Blackwell, 154–76.

Gardner, D. (2005) 'Nexen and the Dictator', 5 November, http://dangardner.ca/nexen-and-the-dictator/

Geiger, D. (2009) Turner in the tropics: the frontier concept revisited (Doctoral dissertation, Verlag nichtermittelbar).

Ghertner, D. (2010) 'Calculating with numbers: Aesthetic governmentality in Delhi's slums', *Economy and Society*, 39(2): 185–217.

Giacomantonio, C. (2014) 'A typology of police organizational boundaries', *Policing and Society*, 24(5): 545–65.

Gill, M. and Hart, J. (1999) 'Private security: Enforcing corporate security policy using private investigators', *European Journal on Criminal Policy and Research*, 7(2): 245–61.

Gilling, D. (2001) 'Community safety and social policy', *European Journal on Criminal Policy and Research*, 9(4): 381–400.

Gilling, D. and Hughes, G. (2002) 'The community safety "profession": Towards a new expertise in the governance of crime, disorder and safety in the UK?', *Safer Communities*, 1(1): 4–12.

Gilling, D., Hughes, G., Bowden, M., Edwards, A., Henry, A. and Topping, J. (2013) 'Powers, liabilities and expertise in community safety: Comparative lessons for "urban security" from the United Kingdom and the Republic of Ireland', *European Journal of Criminology*, 10(3): 326–40.

Globe and Mail (2017) 'Nexen Energy charged after two workers killed in 2016 explosion in Alberta', 27 December, www.theglobeandmail. com/report-on-business/industry-news/energy-and-resources/ nexen-energy-charged-after-two-workers-killed-in-2016-explosion-in-alberta/article37437315/

Goffman, E. (1959) *Presentation of self in everyday life*, New York: Anchor Books.

Goldstein, H. (1990) *Problem-oriented policing*, New York: McGraw-Hill.

Goold, B., Loader, I. and Thumala, A. (2010) 'Consuming security? Tools for a sociology of security consumption', *Theoretical Criminology*, 14(1): 3–30.

Gordon, D. (1998) 'A city beautiful plan for Canada's capital: Edward Bennett and the 1915 plan for Ottawa and Hull', *Planning Perspectives*, 13(3): 275–300.

Graham, S. (2010) *Cities under siege: The new military urbanism*, New York: Verso.

Graycar, A. and Jancsics, D. (2016) 'Gift giving and corruption', *International Journal of Public Administration*, 40(12): 1013–23.

Greene, J. (2014) 'Police research as mastering the tango: The dance and its meanings', in E. Cockbain and J. Knutsson (eds) *Police research: Challenges and opportunities*, London: Routledge, 117–28.

Griffiths, M., Rogers, A. and Anderson, B. (2013) 'Migration, time and temporalities: Review and prospect', COMPAS Research Resources Paper. Centre on Migration Policy and Society.

Guillemin, M. and Gillam, L. (2004) 'Reflexivity and "ethically important moments" in research', *Qualitative Inquiry*, 10(2): 261–80.

Haggerty, K. (2003) 'From risk to precaution: The rationalities of personal crime prevention', in R. Ericson and A. Doyle (eds) *Risk and morality*, Toronto: University of Toronto Press, 193–214.

Haggerty, K. (2004) 'Ethics creep: Governing social science research in the name of ethics', *Qualitative Sociology*, 27(4): 391–414.

Harari, O. and Beaty, D. (1990) 'On the folly of relying solely on a questionnaire methodology in cross-cultural research', *Journal of Managerial Issues*, 2(3): 267–81.

Harcourt, B. (2005) *Illusion of order: The false promise of broken windows policing* (Revised edn), Harvard University Press.

Haywood, J., Kautt, P. and Whitaker, A. (2009) 'The effects of "alley-gating" in an English town', *European Journal of Criminology*, 6(4): 361–81.

Haywood, K. (2004) 'Space – the final frontier: Criminology, the city and the spatial dynamics of exclusion', in J. Ferrell, K. Hayward, W. Morrison and M. Presdee (eds) *Cultural Criminology Unleashed*. London: Glass House Press, 155–66.

Heinis, J. (2016) 'Feds: Ex-Jersey City cop admits accepting $230k as part of corrupt off-duty scheme', https://hudsoncountyview.com/feds-ex-jersey-city-cop-admits-accepting-230k-as-part-of-corrupt-off-duty-scheme/

Helston, C. (2015) 'Retired conservation officer speaks out about the realities of a service stretched too thin', Infonews.ca, https://infotel.ca/newsitem/retired-conservation-officer-speaks-out-about-the-realities-of-a-service-stretched-too-thin/it19294

Herbert, S. (1997) *Policing Space: Territoriality and the Los Angeles Police Department*, Minneapolis: University of Minnesota Press.

Herbert, S. and Beckett, K. (2006) 'Conceptions of space and crime in the punitive neoliberal city', *Antipode*, 38(4): 755–77.

Hermer, J. (1997) 'Keeping Oshawa beautiful: Policing the loiterer in public nuisance By-Law 72-94', *Canadian Journal of Law and Society*, 12(1): 171–92.

Hermer, J. (2002) *The nature of order in North American parks: Regulating Eden*, Toronto: University of Toronto Press.

Hermer, J. and Mosher, J. (2002) *Disorderly people: Law and the politics of exclusion in Ontario*, Halifax: Fernwood Press.

Hermer, J., Kempa, M., Shearing, C., Stenning, P. and Wood, J. (2005) 'Policing in Canada in the twenty-first century: Directions for law reform', in D. Cooley (ed.) *Re-imagining policing in Canada*, Toronto: University of Toronto Press.

Hier, S. and Walby, K. (2014) 'Policy mutations, compliance myths, and re-deployable special event public camera surveillance in Canada', *Sociology*, 48(1): 150–66.

Hodgkinson, S. and Tilley, N. (2011) 'Tackling anti-social behavior: Lessons from new labour for the Coalition government', *Criminology & Criminal Justice*, 11(4): 283–305.

Hoogenboom, B. and Punch, M. (2012) 'Developments in police research: Views from across the North Sea', in T. Newburn and J. Peay (eds) *Policing: Politics, culture, and control. Essays in honour of Robert Reiner*, Oxford: Hart Publishing, 69–88.

Hope, T. (2005) 'The new local governance of community safety in England and Wales', *Canadian Journal of Criminology and Criminal Justice*, 47(2): 369–87.

Hoyt, L. (2003) *The business improvement district: an internationally diffused approach to revitalization*, Washington: International Downtown Association.

Hoyt, L. (2005) 'Do business improvement organizations make a difference?', *Journal of Planning Education and Research*, 25(2): 185–99.

Huey, L. (2007) *Negotiating demands: The politics of skid row policing in Edinburgh, San Francisco, and Vancouver*, Toronto: University of Toronto Press.

Huey, L., Ericson, R. and Haggerty, K. (2005) 'Policing fantasy city', in D. Cooley (ed.) *Reimagining policing in Canada*, Toronto: University of Toronto Press, 140–208.

Hughes, G. and Gilling, D. (2004) '"Mission impossible?" The habitus of the community safety manager and the new expertise in the local partnership governance of crime and safety', *Criminology & Criminal Justice*, 4(2): 129–49.

Hunt, A. and Wickham, G. (1994) *Foucault and law: towards a sociology of law as governance*. London: Pluto Press.

International Downtown Association (2018) 'March Downtown of the Month: Atlanta, GA', www.ida-downtown.org/eweb/dynamicpage. aspx?webcode=dtomatlanta

Jancsics, D. (2017) 'Offshoring at home? Domestic use of shell companies for corruption', *Public Integrity*, 19(1): 4–21.

Jaywork, C. (2017) 'Burgess seeks to clamp down on police moonlighting', www.seattleweekly.com/NEWS/BURGESS-SEEKS-TO-CLAMP-DOWN-ON-POLICE-MOONLIGHTING/

Johnston, L. (1988) 'Controlling police work: problems of organisational reform in large public bureaucracies', *Work, Employment and Society*, 2(1): 51–70.

Johnston, L. (2003) 'From "pluralisation" to "the police extended family": Discourses on the governance of community policing in Britain', *International Journal of the Sociology of Law*, 31(3): 185–204.

Johnston, L. and Shearing, C. (2003) *Governing security: Explorations in policing and justice*, New York: Routledge.

Johnston, L. and Shearing, C. (2010) 'Nodal wars and network fallacies: A genealogical analysis of global insecurities', *Theoretical Criminology*, 14(4): 495–515.

Jones, T. and Newburn, T. (1999) 'Urban change and policing: Mass private property re-considered', *European Journal of Criminal Policy and Research*, 7(2): 225–44.

Jones, T. and Newburn, T. (2002) 'The transformation of policing? Understanding current trends in policing systems', *British Journal of Criminology*, 42(1): 129–46.

Jones, T. and Newburn, T. (2006) 'Understanding plural policing', in T. Jones and T. Newburn (eds) *Plural policing: A comparative perspective*, New York: Routledge.

Jones, T. and Newburn, T. (2007) *Policy transfer and criminal justice*, Maidenhead: McGraw Hill.

Kaiser, K. (2009) 'Protecting respondent confidentiality in qualitative research', *Qualitative Health Research*, 19(11): 1632–41.

Kawash, S. (1998) 'The homeless body', *Public Culture*, 10(2): 319–39.

Kennelly, J. (2015) '"You're making our city look bad": Olympic security, neoliberal urbanization, and homeless youth', *Ethnography*, 16(1): 3–24.

Kinsman, G. (1995) '"Character weakness" and "fruit machines": Towards an analysis of the anti-homosexual security campaign in the Canadian Civil Service', *Labour*, 35:133–61.

Kirby, M. (2015) 'Community safety officers now patrolling', *Thompson Citizen*, 16 June.

Klodawsky, F., Farrell, S. and D'Aubry, T. (2002) 'Images of homelessness in Ottawa: Implications for local politics', *The Canadian Geographer*, 46(2): 126–43.

Kolossov, V. (2005) 'Border studies: Changing perspectives and theoretical approaches', *Geopolitics*, 10(4): 606–32.

Kristof, L. (1959) 'The nature of frontiers and boundaries', *Annals of the Association of American Geographers*, 49(3): 269–82.

Lamb, G., van der Spuy, E. and Shearing, C. (2018) 'Policing, Boundaries and Police Frontierism'

Lambert, E., Wu, Y., Elechi, O. and Jiang, S. (2012) 'Correlates of support for community-police partnerships in policing among Nigerian and US college students', *International Criminal Justice Review*, 22(3): 276–96.

Langley Times (2010) 'Police host owners', *Langley Times*, 16 February.

Lewis, M. (2017) 'Memo: Seattle officer bragged that 'mini Mafia' controlled off-duty contracts', www.palmbeachpost.com/news/memo-seattle-officer-bragged-that-mini-mafia-controlled-off-duty-contracts/YwTB89zkTi7Dv9GHQPze3N/

Liebowitz, D. and Simon, T. (2002) 'Plans in time', *American Planning Association Journal*, 68(2): 128–31.

Lippert, R. (2007) 'Urban revitalization, security and knowledge transfer: The case of broken windows and kiddie bars', *Canadian Journal of Law and Society*, 22(2): 29–54.

Lippert, R. (2010) 'Mundane and mutant devices of power: Sanctuaries and Business Improvement Districts', *European Journal of Cultural Studies*, 13(4): 477–94.

Lippert, R. and O'Connor, D. (2003) 'Security assemblages: airport security, flexible work and liberal governance', *Alternatives: Local, Global, Political*, 28(3): 331–58.

Lippert, R. and O'Connor, D. (2006) 'Security intelligence networks and the transformation of contract private security', *Policing and Society*, 16(1): 50–66.

Lippert, R. and Walby, K. (2012) 'Municipal corporate security and the intensification of urban surveillance', *Surveillance and Society*, 9(3): 310–20.

Lippert, R. and Walby, K. (2013) (eds) *Policing cities: Urban securitization and regulation in a 21st Century World,* London: Routledge.

Lippert, R. and Walby, K. (2014) 'Marketization, knowledge work, and "users pay" policing in Canada', *British Journal of Criminology*, 54(2): 260–80.

Lippert, R. and Walby, K. (2017) 'Funnelling through foundations and Crime Stoppers: How public police create and span inter-organisational boundaries', *Policing and Society*, 27(6): 602–19.

Lippert, R., Walby, K. and Steckle, R. (2013) 'Multiplicities of corporate security: Identifying emerging types and trends', *Security Journal*, 26(3): 206–21.

Lippert, R., Walby, K. and Taylor, P. (2016) 'Security networks, capital exchanges, and user pays policing', *Criminology, Criminal Justice, Law and Society*, 17(2): 18–33.

Lisle, D. (2014) 'Rejuvenating method', *Critical Studies on Security*, 2(3): 370–3.

Loader, I. (1999) 'Consumer culture and the commodification of policing and security', *Sociology*, 33(2): 373–92.

Loader, I. and Walker, N. (2007) *Civilizing security.* Cambridge: Cambridge University Press.

Loader, I. and White, A. (2018) 'Valour for money? Contested commodification in the market for security', *British Journal of Criminology*, https://doi.org/10.1093/bjc/azy004

Mackin, B. (2016) 'More combat training for BC's natural resource officers', *The Tyee*, 25 May.

Malachowski, C. (2015) 'Organizational culture shock: Ethnographic fieldwork strategies for the novice health science researcher', *Forum: Qualitative Social Research*, 16(2): Art. 9.

Mangelsdorf, R. (2013) 'Foundation gives back to DPD', *South Delta Leader*, 12 April.

Manning, P. (1977) *Police work: The social organization of policing*, Cambridge, MA: MIT Press.

Marcuse, P. (2004) 'The "war on terrorism" and life in cities after September 11, 2001', in S. Graham (ed.) *Cities, war, and terrorism*, Oxford: Blackwell.

Marketwire Canada (2011) 'London drugs pays tribute to the Vancouver Police Foundation', *Comtex New Network*, 24 June.

Marquadt, N. and Füller, H. (2012) 'Spillover of the private city: BIDs as a pivot of social control in downtown Los Angeles', *European Urban and Regional Studies*, 19(2): 153–66.

Martel, J. (2004) 'Policing criminological knowledge: The hazards of qualitative research on women in prison', *Theoretical Criminology*, 8(2): 157–89.

Marx, G. (1984) 'Notes on the discovery, collection, and assessment of hidden and dirty data', in J. Schneider and J. Kitsuse (eds) *Studies in the sociology of social problems*, Norwood, NJ: Ablex, 78–113.

Mawani, R. (2003) 'Imperial legacies (post) colonial identities: Law, space and the making of Stanley Park, 1859-2001', *Law Text Culture*, 7: 98–141.

McAra, L. (2008) 'Crime, criminology and criminal justice in Scotland', *European Journal of Criminology*, 5(4): 481–504.

McCann, E. (2008) 'Expertise, truth, and urban policy mobilities: Global circuits of knowledge in the development of Vancouver, Canada's "four pillar" drug strategy', *Environment and Planning A*, 40(4): 885–904.

McCulloch, J. (2004) 'Blue armies, khaki police and the cavalry on the new American frontier: Critical criminology for the 21st century', *Critical Criminology*, 12(3): 309-326.

McDonald, D. C. (1979) *The commission of inquiry concerning certain activities of the Royal Canadian Mounted Police. First Report*, Ottawa: Supply and Services Canada.

McDonald, S. (2005) 'Studying actions in context: A qualitative shadowing method for organizational research', *Qualitative Research*, 5(4): 455–73.

McDonald, T. (2017a) 'What we know about the federal probe of Jersey City police', www.nj.com/hudson/index.ssf/2017/01/what_you_should_know_about_the_jersey_city_off-dut.html

McDonald, T. (2017b) 'Jersey City cop admits taking $55K in off-duty jobs scheme', www.nj.com/hudson/index.ssf/2017/06/jersey_city_cop_pleads_guilty_to_federal_bribery_c.html

McDonald, T. (2017c) 'Jersey City mayor faces police ire over halting off-duty jobs', www.nj.com/hudson/index.ssf/2018/01/jersey_city_mayor_faces_police_ire_over_halting_of.html

McDonald, T. (2017d) '3 more cops face prison in federal probe of Jersey City police', www.nj.com/hudson/index.ssf/2017/07/number_of_guilty_pleas_in_federal_probe_of_jersey.html

McDonald, T. (2018) 'Jersey City moves to ax off-duty jobs for cops', www.nj.com/hudson/index.ssf/2018/02/jersey_city_moves_to_ax_off-duty_jobs_for_cops.html

McDonald, W.F. (1995) 'The globalization of criminology: The new frontier is the frontier', *Transnational Organized Crime*, 1(1): 1–22.

Mertz, E. (2018) 'Nexen pleads guilty, fined $460K for 2015 Long Lake pipeline spill', Global News, 13 July, https://globalnews.ca/news/4331126/nexen-long-lake-oil-spill-guilty-fine/

Millie, A. (2008) 'Anti-social behavior, behavioral expectations and an urban aesthetic', *British Journal of Criminology*, 48(3): 379–94.

Millie, A. (2016) 'Urban Interventionism as a challenge to aesthetic order: Towards an aesthetic criminology', *Crime, Media, Culture*, 13(1): 3–20.

Milwaukee Downtown (2018) 'Public service ambassadors', www.milwaukeedowntown.com/about-us/bid-21-programs/public-service-ambassadors

Mintrom, M. (1997) 'Policy entrepreneurs and the diffusion of innovation', *American Journal of Political Science*, 41(3): 738–70.

Miraftab, F. (2007) 'Governing post-Apartheid spatiality: Implementing city improvement districts in Cape Town', *Antipode*, 39(4): 602–26.

Mitchell, D. (1997) 'The annihilation of space by law: The roots and implications of anti-homeless laws in the United States', *Antipode*, 29(3): 303–35.

Mitchell, D. (2003) *The right to the city: Social justice and the fight for public space*, New York: Guilford.

Mitchell, D. and Staeheli, L. (2006) 'Clean and safe? Property redevelopment, public space and homelessness in downtown San Diego', in S. Low and N. Smith (eds) *The politics of public space*, London: Routledge, 143–76.

Monaghan, J. (2013) 'Mounties in the frontier: Circulations, anxieties, and myths of settler colonialism', *Journal of Canadian Studies*, 47(1): 122–48.

Monaghan, R. (2008) 'Community-based justice in Northern Ireland and South Africa', *International Criminal Justice Review*, 18(1): 83–105.

Mopas, M. and Stenning, P. (2001) 'Tools of the trade: the symbolic power of private security: An exploratory study', *Policing and Society*, 11(1): 67–97.

Moran-Ellis, J., Alexander, V., Cronin, A., Dickinson, M., Fielding, J., Sleney, J. and Thomas, H. (2006) 'Triangulation and integration: Processes, claims and implications', *Qualitative Research*, 6(1): 45–59.

Municipal Insurance Association of British Columbia (MIABC) (2004) 'Partners in risk management', Vancouver: MIABC.

Murphy, C. (1998) 'The development, impact and implications of community policing in Canada', in S. Mastrofski and J. Green (eds) *Community policing reality or rhetoric*, Thousand Oaks: Sage, 178–89.

Murphy, S. (2009) '"Compassionate" strategies of managing homelessness: Post-revanchist geographies in San Francisco', *Antipode*, 41(2): 305–25.

Mynorthwest.com (2017) 'Seattle Mayor Burgess seeks to regulate off duty police jobs', http://mynorthwest.com/766717/burgess-task-force-on-seattle-police/

Nalla, M. and Hummer, D. (1999) 'Relations between police officers and security professionals: A study of perceptions', *Security Journal*, 12(3): 31–40.

National Capital Commission (1965) 'An account of the history, legislation and composition of the National Capital Commission together with an outline of the work, projects and other functions of the commission', Ottawa: Information Division of the National Capital Commission.

Naum, M. (2010) 'Re-emerging frontiers: Postcolonial theory and historical archaeology of the borderlands', *Journal of Archaeological Method and Theory*, 17(2): 101–31.

Nettelbeck, A. (2011) 'The Australian frontier in the museum', *Journal of Social History*, 44(4): 1115–28.

Nettelbeck, A. and Smandych, R. (2010) 'Policing indigenous peoples on two colonial frontiers: Australia's mounted police and Canada's North-West Mounted Police', *Australian & New Zealand Journal of Criminology*, 43(2): 356–75.

Newburn, T. (2001) 'The commodification of policing: security networks in the late modern city', *Urban Studies*, 38(5/6): 829–48.

Newman, D. (2003) 'On borders and power: A theoretical framework', *Journal of Borderlands Studies*, 18(1): 13–25.

Newman, D. (2006) 'Borders and bordering towards an interdisciplinary dialogue', *European Journal of Social Theory*, 9(2): 171–86.

News12 New Jersey (2018) 'Jersey City puts end to police officers working off-duty jobs', http://newjersey.news12.com/story/37409999/jersey-city-puts-end-to-police-officers-working-off-duty-jobs

Nguyen, K. (2015) 'New community safety officers hit the streets', *paNOW*, 10 August.

Nicholson-Crotty, S. (2009) 'The politics of diffusion: Public policy in the American states', *The Journal of Politics*, 71(1): 192–205.

O'Malley, P. and Hutchinson, S. (2007) 'Converging corporatization? Police management, police unionism, and the transfer of business principles', *Police Practice and Research*, 8(2): 159–74.

Ontario Provincial Police Museum (OPP Museum) (2014) *Behind the badge: The story of the Ontario Provincial Police*. Gallery Guide. Queens Printer.

Park, G. and Lippert, R. (2008) 'Legal aid's logics', *Studies in Law, Politics and Society*, 45: 177–201.

Parker, N. and Vaughan-Williams, N. (2012) 'Critical border studies: Broadening and deepening the 'lines in the sand' agenda', *Geopolitics*, 17(4): 727–33.

Peck, J. (2011) 'Geographies of policy: From transfer-diffusion to mobility-mutation', *Progress in Human Geography*, 35(6): 773–97.

Peck, J. and Theodore, N. (2010) 'Mobilizing policy: Models, methods, and mutations', *Geoforum*, 41(2): 169–74.

Penders, B., Verbakel, J. and Nelis, A. (2009) 'The social study of corporate science: A research manifesto', *Bulletin of Science, Technology and Society*, 29(6): 439–46.

Pendleton, M. (1998) 'Policing the park: Understanding soft enforcement', *Journal of Leisure Research*, 30(4): 552–71.

Pendleton, M. (2000) 'Leisure, crime and cops: Exploring a paradox of our civility', *Journal of Leisure Research*, 32(1): 111–15.

Peršak, N. (2016) 'Criminalising through the back door: normative grounds and social accounts of the incivilities regulation', in N. Peršak (ed.) *Regulation and social control of incivilities*, London, New York: Routledge, 13–34.

Peyroux, E., Pütz, R. and Glasze, G. (2012) 'Business improvement districts (BIDs): Internationalisation and contextualisation of a "travelling concept"', *European Urban and Regional Studies*, 19(2): 111–20.

Pitt Meadows Times (2008) 'Community safety officers set to hit the streets', *Putt Meadows Times*, 11 July.

Post-Tribune (2015) 'New off-duty work policy a problem, Gary cops say', *Chicago Tribune*, 11 June.

Power, M. (2004) 'Counting, control and calculation: reflections on measuring and management', *Human Relations*, 57(6): 765–83.

Pratt, A. (2017) 'The Canada-US Shiprider Programme, jurisdiction and the crime-security nexus', in R. Lippert, K. Walby, I. Warren and D. Palmer (eds) *National security, surveillance and terror: Canada and Australia in comparative perspective,* Palgrave Macmillan, 249–72.

Prior, L. (2010) 'Qualitative research design and ethical governance: Some problems of fit', *Ethics Forum*, 12: 53–64.

Public Interest Law Centre (2007) 'Panhandling in Winnipeg: Legislation versus support services', Volume 4. Public Interest Law Centre. University of Winnipeg, Winnipeg, Manitoba.

Pue, W. (2000) (ed.) *Pepper in our eyes*, Vancouver: UBC Press.

Pulkkinen, L. (2017) 'Chief: I gave complaints about moonlighting Seattle cops to FBI', https://www.seattlepi.com/seattlenews/article/Chief-I-gave-complaints-about-Seattle-cops-12216288.php

Riach, K. (2009) 'Exploring participant-centered reflexivity in the research interview', *Sociology*, 43(2): 356–70.

Rigakos, G. (2002) *The new parapolice: Risk markets and commodified social control*, Toronto: University of Toronto Press.

Robertson, J. (2013) 'Police cost a sour note at concerts', *Sydney Morning Herald*, 11 September.

Rose, N. (2000) 'Governing cities, governing citizens', in E. Isin (ed.) *Democracy, citizenship, and the global city*, London: Routledge.

Rose, N. and Miller, P. (1992) 'Political power beyond the state: problematics of government', *British Journal of Sociology*, 43(2): 172–205.

Rose, N., O'Malley, P. and Valverde, M. (2006) 'Governmentality', *Annual Review of Law and Social Science*, 2: 83–104.

Royal Canadian Mounted Police (RCMP) (2012) 'Community safety officer pilot program evaluation report', www.rcmp-grc.gc.ca/aud-ver/reports-rapports/ppcso-asc-eval-eng.htm

Royal Canadian Mounted Police (RCMP) (2018a) 'Feature Gallery', http://rcmphc.com/exhibits-2/

Royal Canadian Mounted Police (RCMP) (2018b) 'Self-guided tour', http://rcmphc.wpengine.com/wp-content/uploads/2016/04/RCMP-HC-Self-Guided-Tour-Brochure-web-2016.pdf

Rumford, C. (2008) 'Introduction: citizens and borderwork in Europe', *Space and Polity*, 12(1): 1–12.

Sarre, R. and Prenzler, T. (2000) 'The relationship between police and private security: Models and future directions', *International Journal of Comparative and Applied Criminal Justice*, 24(1): 91–113.

Savage, M. and Burrows, R. (2007) 'The coming crisis of empirical sociology', *Sociology*, 41(5): 885–899.

Schwalbe, M. and Wolkomir, M. (2001) 'The masculine self as problem and resource in interview studies of men', *Men and Masculinities*, 4(1): 90–103.

Scott, J., Hogg, R., Barclay, E. and Donnermeyer, J. (2007) 'There's crime out there, but not as we know it: Rural criminology – the last frontier', in E. Barclay, J. Donnermeyer, J. Scott and R. Hogg (eds) *Crime in rural Australia*. Annandale, NSW: Federation Press.

Shearing, C. (1992) 'The relation between public and private policing', *Crime and Justice*, 15: 399–434.

Shearing, C. and Stenning, P. (1981) 'Modern private security: Its growth and implications', *Crime and Justice*, 3: 193–245.

Shearing, C. and Stenning, P. (1985) 'From the panopticon to Disney World: The development of discipline', in A. Doob and E. Greenspan (eds) *Perspectives in criminal law Ontario*, Canada Law Book Inc., 335–49.

Shearing, C. and Wood, J. (2003) 'Governing security for common goods', *International Journal of the Sociology of Law*, 31: 205–25.

Shepherdson, P., Clancey, G., Lee, M. and Crofts, T. (2014) 'Community safety and crime prevention partnerships: Challenges and opportunities', *International Journal for Crime, Justice and Social Democracy*, 3(1): 107–20.

Sleiman, M. and Lippert, R. (2010) 'Downtown ambassadors, police relations and "clean and safe" security', *Policing and Society*, 20(3): 316–35.

Smith, N. (1996) *The new urban frontier: Gentrification and the revanchist city*, New York: Routledge.

Smith, N. (2001) 'Global social cleansing: Post-liberal revanchism and the export of zero tolerance', *Social Justice*, 28(3): 68–74.

Statistics Canada (2012) 'Aboriginal peoples in Canada: First Nations people, Metis and Inuit', Census product 99-011-X.

Stenning, P. (2000) 'Powers and accountability of private police', *European Journal on Criminal Policy and Research*, 8(3): 325–52.

Stoughton, S. (2017) 'Moonlighting: The private employment of off-duty officers', *Indiana Law Review*, 5: 1847–1900.

Thomas, G. (2014) 'Research on policing: Insights from the literature', *Police Journal: Theory, Practice and Principles*, 87: 5–16.

Thomas, N. (2011) 'Thirty years after the bathhouse raids', *Toronto Star*, 4 February.

Thompson Citizen (2016) 'Positive signs from first year of Community Safety Officer Program', *Thompson Citizen*, 24 August.

Thumala, A., Goold, B. and Loader, I. (2011) 'A tainted trade? Moral ambivalence and legitimation work in the private security industry', *British Journal of Sociology*, 62(2): 283–303.

Tracey, S. (2010) 'Qualitative quality: Eight "big-tent" criteria for excellent qualitative research', *Qualitative Inquiry*, 16(10): 837–49.

Tyler, T. (2004) 'Enhancing police legitimacy', *The Annals of the American Academy of Political and Social Science*, 593(1): 84–99.

Valverde, M. (2003) *Law's dream of a common knowledge*, Princeton: Princeton University Press.

Valverde, M. (2005) 'Taking "land use" seriously: Toward an ontology of municipal law', *Law Text Culture*, 9(1): 34–59.

Valverde, M. (2008) 'The ethic of diversity: Local law and the negotiation of urban norms', *Law and Social Inquiry*, 33(4): 895–923.

Valverde, M. (2009) 'Jurisdiction and scale: Legal "technicalities" as resources for theory', *Social and Legal Studies*, 18(2): 139–57.

Valverde, M. (2010) *The force of law*, Toronto: Groundwood Books.

Vancouver Police Foundation (2014) 'Police Sunglasses Raise Funds for Community Outreach Programs', http://mediareleases.vpd.ca/2014/06/16/police-sunglasses-raise-funds-for-community-outreach-programs/

Victoria Times Colonist (2006) 'Langford Mulls municipal security patrol', *Victoria Times Colonist*, 8 February.

Vindevogel, F. (2005) 'Private security and urban crime mitigation: A bid for BIDs', *Criminology & Criminal Justice*, 5(3): 233–55.

Virta, S. (2002) 'Local security management: policing through networks', *Policing*, 25(1): 190–200.

von Mahs, J. (2005) 'The sociospatial exclusion of single homeless people in Berlin and Los Angeles', *American Behavioral Scientist*, 48(8): 928–60.

Wakin, M. (2008) 'Using vehicles to challenge antisleeping ordinances', *City and Community*, 7(4): 309–29.

Walby, K. (2007) 'Contributions to a post-sovereigntist understanding of law: Foucault, law as governance, and legal pluralism', *Social and Legal Studies*, 16(3): 551–71.

Walby, K. (2009) '"He asked me if I was looking for fags…" Ottawa's National Capital Commission conservation officers and the policing of public park sex', *Surveillance and Society*, 6(4): 367–79.

Walby, K. and Larsen, M. (2012) 'Access to information and freedom of information requests: Neglected means of data production in the social sciences', *Qualitative Inquiry*, 18(1): 31–42.

Walby, K. and Lippert, R. (2012) 'The new keys to the city: Uploading corporate security and threat discourse into Canadian municipal governments', *Crime, Law and Social Change*, 58(4): 437–55.

Walby, K. and Lippert, R. (2013) 'Municipal corporate security and risk mitigation in Canadian cities', in R. Lippert and K. Walby (eds) *Policing cities: Urban securitization and regulation in 21st century cities*, London: Routledge, 207–21.

Walby, K. and Lippert, R. (2015a) *Municipal corporate security in international context*, London: Routledge.

Walby, K. and Lippert, R. (2015b) 'Ford First? Corporate Security and the US Department of Wars Plant Protection Services Interior Organization Unit 1917-1918', *Labor History*, 56(2): 117–35.

Walby, K., Lippert, R. and Gacek, J. (2017) 'Securitising National Interests: Canadian Federal Government Departments, Corporate Security Creep, and Security Regimes', in R. Lippert, K. Walby, I. Warren, and D. Palmer (eds) *National security, surveillance, and terror: Canada and Australia in comparative perspective*, London: Palgrave-MacMillan, 155–76.

Walby, K. and Monaghan, J. (2010) 'Policing proliferation: On the militarization of police and Atomic Energy Canada Limited's nuclear response forces', *Canadian Journal of Criminology and Criminal Justice*, 52(2): 117–45.

Walby, K., Wilkinson, B. and Lippert, R. (2016) 'Legitimacy, professionalization, and expertise in public sector corporate security', *Policing and Society*, 26(1): 38–54.

Ward, K. (2007) '"Policies in motion", urban management and state restructuring: The trans-local expansion of Business Improvement Districts', *International Journal of Urban and Regional Research*, 30(1): 54–75.

Weber, M. (1946 [1922]) 'Bureaucracy', in H. Gerth and C.W. Mills (eds) *From Max Weber: Essays in sociology*, New York: Oxford University Press, 196–244

Weiss, R. (2014) 'Corporate security at Ford Motor Company: From the Great War to the Cold War', in K. Walby and R. Lippert (eds) *Corporate security in the 21st century: Theory and practice in international perspective*, London: Palgrave Macmillan, 17–38.

Welch, M. (2012) 'The sonics of crimmigration in Australia: Wall of noise and quiet manoeuvring', *British Journal of Criminology*, 52(2): 324–34.

White, A. (2010) *The politics of private security*, London: Palgrave MacMillan.

White, A. (2015) 'The politics of police "privatization": A multiple streams approach', *Criminology & Criminal Justice*, 15(3): 283–99.

Williams, C. (2008) 'Constables for hire: the history of private 'public' policing in the UK. *Policing and Society*, 18(2): 190–205

Williams, J. (2005) 'The politics of homelessness: Shelter now and political protest', *Political Research Quarterly*, 58(3): 497–509.

Wilson, D. (2004) 'Toward a contingent urban neoliberalism', *Urban Geography*, 25(8): 771–83.

Wilson, J. and Kelling, G. (1982) 'Broken windows: The police and neighborhood safety', *The Atlantic Monthly*, March: 29–37.

Winnipeg BIZ (2018) 'We're hiring. Join the exchange patrol', Unpublished advertisement.

Witsil, F. (2015) 'Detroit ambassadors sworn in, aim to make city inviting', *Detroit Free Press*, 11 June.

Wood, J. and Dupont, B. (eds) (2006) *Democracy, society and the governance of security*, Cambridge: Cambridge University Press.

Wood, J. and Shearing, C. (2006) *Imagining security*, Cullompton: Willan.

Zedner, L. (2007) 'Pre-crime and post-criminology?', *Theoretical Criminology*, 11(2): 261–81.

Zukin, S. (2010) *Naked city: The death and life of authentic urban places*, New York: Oxford University Press.

Index